Supporting Struggling Readers

BARBARA J. WALKER

Pippin Publishing

Designed by John Zehethofer
Edited by Dyanne Rivers
Printed and bound in Canada by AGMV Marquis Imprimeur Inc.

We acknowledge the financial support of the Government of Canada
through the Book Publishing Industry Development Program for our
publishing activities.

We acknowledge the support of the Government of Ontario through the
Ontario Media Development Corporation's Ontario Book Initiative.

National Library of Canada Cataloguing in Publication

Walker, Barbara J., 1946-
    Supporting struggling readers / Barbara J. Walker; edited by Dyanne
Rivers. —2nd ed., rev. and expanded

(Pippin teacher's library ; 41)
Includes bibliographical references.
ISBN 0-88751-086-8 (pbk.)

1. Reading — Remedial teaching. I. Rivers, Dyanne. II. Title.
III. Series.

LB1050.5.W355 2003   372.43   C2003-905183-8

10 9 8 7 6 5 4 3 2

CONTENTS

INTRODUCTION

Readers of all descriptions work to make sense of the literacy events that crowd their lives. Struggling readers, too, work to make sense of literacy events, often in situations that inhibit, rather than support, their search for meaning. Nevertheless, they *are* active learners in search of meaning who deserve support as they struggle to make sense.

To help you understand and support their literacy development, this book will illustrate:

— An interactive view of the reading process.
— A developmental view of literacy.
— How inappropriate instruction can affect students' strengths and weaknesses and reinforce their reliance on ineffective learning strategies.
— Instructional methods and authentic assessment procedures that enable us to support struggling readers as they develop their literacy skills.
— An instructional framework that can be used to intervene effectively during each phase of literacy development.

In the years since this book was first published, teaching strategies and techniques have been refined and adapted to reflect new developments in the field of literacy instruction. As a result, this new, revised edition of *Supporting Struggling Readers* includes even more suggestions for helping children whose literacy development has stalled.

Furthermore, my continuing work in the field has sparked me to rework, update and shift to different chapters some of the teaching strategies included in the original edition. Though all the suggested strategies can be adapted for use at every phase of a child's literacy development, many are particularly effective when matched with specific developmental tasks. Two strategies included in the chapter dealing with strategic literacy, for example, are the directed reading-thinking activity and the experience-text relationship. They appear in this chapter because they focus on helping children integrate and elaborate on their previous knowledge as they read a text, the major developmental task of the strategic literacy phase. Both strategies can, however, also be used effectively to promote literacy development during other phases.

New teaching strategies have been added throughout the book to reflect research suggesting that word identification skills and the ability to read fluently are important elements of comprehension. We must remember, however, that children who are at risk of failing to learn to read proficiently struggle with these elements of the comprehension process. Emphasizing these strategies at the expense of strategies that encourage children to make sense when reading prevents struggling readers from demonstrating what they can do.

As you read this new edition, I hope that you will come to appreciate that struggling readers do attempt to make sense of what they read and that they do so by drawing on what they can already do. Too often, instruction focuses on what they can't do, leaving them struggling to make sense of what they're reading and writing. If teachers support the literacy development of struggling readers by joining them in focusing on what they can do, they are able to successfully construct meaning from text.

. . . .

ACTIVE LITERACY

Being literate means that children and adults are able to use reading and writing to make sense of their world. But literacy development now involves far more than the ability to pick up a book and read — or to pick up a pencil and write. Advances in technology, especially computer technology, have added layers of complexity to the definition of literacy. In addition to reading and writing using traditional print materials, students must now know how to read and write material that is generated electronically, such as Web pages, e-mail correspondence and chatroom messages. All involve different aspects of literacy.

As we read and discuss with one another, we use a multitude of strategies depending on the situation. Our purposes for reading affect both the strategies we use and our interpretation of the text. Take the case, for example, of a young man who was reading a manual as he repaired a motor in auto mechanics class. He read a few paragraphs, looked at a diagram, then worked on the engine. Later that day, he sat reading a movie magazine for his own enjoyment. As he read, he decided that his friends might be interested in hearing about and discussing some of the information in the article.

The reading strategies the young man used on these two occasions changed because his purpose had changed — from reading to perform a task to reading for enjoyment and, finally, to reading so that he would be able to recount a specific point. Readers also vary their strategies as the text organization changes. In the case of the young man, for example, the text changed from a manual with diagrams to a magazine designed for leisure reading.

Because readers' knowledge of various topics differs, their level of understanding changes with the topic. As the young man read the auto manual, he understood most of what he was reading and simply read to confirm or add to information he already knew. As he read the movie magazine, he read quickly at first. When he decided that he wanted to discuss the information with friends, however, he not only slowed down, but also reread sections. He wanted to be sure that he understood the author's perspective, which gave him new information, so that he could contrast it with his own.

In the same way, a group of children from Calgary, Alberta, read and understood a difficult passage about glaciers because they had just returned from an excursion to the Columbia Icefields where they had seen firsthand how glaciers form. This same group of children, however, had great difficulty when they read an easier passage about tropical rain forests. In these two instances, the students had not changed — but the text had. They had trouble interpreting the passage about rain forests because they weren't familiar with the topic.

In most cases, reading difficulties are not the result of an underlying cognitive deficit in a reader; rather, a reader's ability to make sense of text depends on the complex interaction of myriad factors — the strategies they possess, their purpose for reading, their knowledge of the topic, the format of the text, and the situational context. The ability — or inability — to read is not a static characteristic; rather, it is contingent on the interaction among a unique reader, a text and instruction. Both the reader's ability and the difficulty of a literacy activity are relative. This chapter examines how reading proficiency develops by taking a closer look at the active process of making sense of text — a process that involves readers in predicting, checking and elaborating on their interpretation within a particular situation.

Predicting

Proficient readers use what they already know to predict what a text will say. They use this strategy, as well as the information given in a text, to make sense of a passage. As they read, their previous knowledge helps them recognize patterns that give them clues about how to interpret a text. Just as a weather forecaster uses an array of instruments to predict the weather, readers use an array of information sources to predict what a text is likely to say. These information sources, such as the features and meaning of words, sentence organization and the organization of the text, combine with readers' previous knowledge about words and their familiarity with the topic to facilitate understanding.

When reading a passage about a roller coaster ride, for example, readers might say to themselves, I know what this is going to say, because I've ridden a roller coaster. In this way, their personal experience with riding a roller coaster enables them to predict what the text is going to say. Like the weather forecaster's predictions, however, theirs are sometimes accurate — and sometimes not.

Checking Predictions

Active literacy involves not only making predictions, but also checking those predictions. Proficient readers continually check their understanding of a passage to see whether it makes sense. As they read more text about the roller coaster ride, for example, they might say to themselves, Yes, that is exactly how I felt when I rode the roller coaster, or, Oops, this character didn't have the same experience as I did.

This internal dialogue enables readers to monitor their understanding. If they are having trouble understanding, they check both the text and their own previous knowledge to figure out what went wrong. Then, they revise their understanding and continue to read. Like the weather forecaster, they continually check data from a variety of sources, revising and refining their original predictions.

Developing readers check their understanding by asking themselves questions that direct their use of fix-up strategies. They reread to correct misunderstandings or check their own previous knowledge. As this active process of predicting and revising continues, children begin to reflect on the topic they're reading about, the structure of the text, and the strategies they're using. This leads to further development of literacy.

Elaborating on Strategies and Understanding

As students read and write, they elaborate on what and how they read. About the roller coaster passage, for example, they might say to themselves: Hey, I get this because it's like the octopus ride at the fair. They make associations between what they already know and the new information in the passage — and these new associations become part of what they know.

Just as weather forecasters encounter new phenomena and identify their particular patterns, readers, too, identify patterns as they read. When they see a particular pattern for a second or third time, both readers and weather forecasters describe this pattern so they can recognize it quickly in subsequent experiences.

As readers augment their knowledge of a topic or strategy, they think about how the new knowledge jibes with what they already know and do. Thus, by engaging in literacy activities, readers learn to connect patterns in text with their own knowledge. When these patterns are encountered frequently, they are refined and integrated into what readers already know. In subsequent literacy experiences, they use this information or strategy more readily because it has become familiar. In this way, frequent reading and writing become tools for connecting what students know and do, helping to build a network of information sources and decoding strategies.

Situating Literacy

Readers are constantly expanding their repertoire of strategies for dealing with text. As they do so, they think about the situation in which the literacy event occurred, another characteristic of active literacy. The social aspects of literacy influence developing readers' attitudes, their definition of literacy, and the strategies they use. For example, a young child listening to a parent read a story is involved in a social experience that transfers meaning to printed language. The parent conveys meaning by reading with expression and emotion. As the parent and child talk about the words on the page, they create a social interaction that affects the child's perceptions of literacy.

These same interactions continue into the culture of the school. In fact, school has become a culture of its own. Like parents, teachers are an integral part of the literacy context, orchestrating it and negotiating meaning among class members. For example, one struggling eight-year-old asked her teacher, "When do I get out of the group with all the boys?" Her membership in this group of readers experiencing difficulty was limiting her reading development, as well as that of the boys. This anecdote illustrates that the circumstances in which reading occurs can influence developing readers' purposes and their perspectives on literacy events.

Another example involves a young student in a foods class. She became involved in writing a report on lime. However, she forgot to check the context and wrote an extensive report on lime, the stone. The next day, she walked into the foods class, assessed the context, and realized that the report should have been on lime, the fruit.

Readers constantly use their knowledge of the situation to select both the strategies and the information they use. Thus, circumstances affect what developing readers perceive as important, how sources are combined, what is elaborated on and how strategies are selected, as well as their perceptions about the literacy event.

The Reading Process

This model shows how the previously discussed aspects of the reading process interact continuously as developing readers construct meaning.

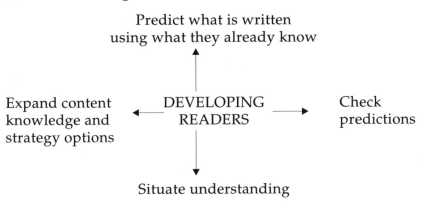

13

Developing readers predict what the text will say by linking sources of information (previous knowledge and the text) and checking — and revising when necessary — their predictions and interpretations. As they read, they add to their knowledge of the topic and elaborate on the strategies they use. Within each literacy event, knowledge is reconstructed as the learner reflects on how a particular context affected his interpretation. As students read and write, resolving ambiguities in a variety of literacy contexts, they refine and generalize their knowledge and strategies. As a result, these are constantly evolving.

Summary

An interactive view of reading involves four important principles:

- Developing readers use many sources of information to predict what a text will say.
- Developing readers automatically monitor their interpretation of a text by checking their predictions against the text to figure out what makes sense.
- Developing readers expand their content knowledge and strategy options by embedding new information and strategies within existing knowledge.
- Developing readers select strategies and expand their knowledge of a topic depending on the situation — academic, recreational, etc. — they encounter.

. . . .

REASONS

FOR READING DIFFICULTY

All readers use what they can already do to work out difficulties they encounter as they read and write. When a task calls for them to use strategies that are unfamiliar or that they can't perform, they avoid these. Instead, they fall back on what they can already do. For this reason, readers who are continually placed in situations where learning is difficult develop inappropriate compensatory strategies. Rather than double-checking the text, for example, some will guess wildly at words, using what they think the text might say and sometimes actually creating a new story. Others, who are unfamiliar with a topic, will read strings of words, hoping to find something that makes sense. They don't check their own knowledge to look for ways to connect what they're reading to what they already know. Their use of these inappropriate alternative strategies often causes parents and teachers to view these students as less able to engage in literacy activities.

Believing these students to be less capable, teachers often reduce the quantity and quality of instruction, increasing the likelihood that they will be placed in learning situations where they'll develop inappropriate compensatory strategies. And so the cycle continues.

When students repeatedly find themselves in situations where their natural sense-making strategies are at odds with the instruction they receive, they begin to rely solely on inappropriate alternative strategies to construct meaning. This reliance hinders their literacy development and their reading becomes unproductive. For example, beginning readers who rely on their personal knowledge rather than textual clues may be fairly successful — at first. Eventually, however, they'll find themselves in situations where they must make predictions using their personal knowledge, then check their predictions against words in the text. If they're inattentive and randomly select letters when doing this checking, they'll find that the strategy doesn't work. As a result, they will abandon it in favor of relying on their personal knowledge and, perhaps, the clues they get from pictures. In other words, they will shift away from a particular information source rather than integrating and linking it with other sources. This will prevent them from developing more flexible strategies.

As indicated by this example, the interactive model of reading can set up a framework for studying reading difficulty. Reading difficulty develops when students frequently rely on a single source of information rather than linking sources, repeatedly read difficult passages that restrict the growth of knowledge and strategies, read without checking meaning, a practice that results in the development of limited rather than flexible strategies, and expect literacy activities to result in failure. Thus, reading difficulty is not a static characteristic that lies solely within the student; rather, it is influenced by a variety of factors that interact during each literacy event.

Difficulty Linking Sources of Information

At the onset of literacy, children learn to link sources of information. Often, however, struggling readers exhibit a deficiency in either a skill, such as sight-word knowledge, or an ability, such as sound blending, that causes them to shift away from an information source.

In an essay in the *Handbook of Reading Research*, Richard Allington says, "Poor beginning readers ... seem to rely on one available source of information rather than integrating all available cues." These readers experience difficulty because they don't link sources of information. For example, readers who have difficulty with sound blending may try to decode an unfamiliar word by relying on what they know about the picture rather than sounding out the letters . When the topic is familiar, this strategy may be productive. When these readers confront unfamiliar topics and avoid looking at the text to sound out a few letters in the word, however, their interpretation becomes increasingly muddled. By relying solely on what they can already do — using background knowledge, in this instance — they develop inappropriate strategies. In essence, a strength becomes a weakness.

Here's another example. Sandy had trouble learning the sounds of letters in his first year of school. Although he had had a wealth of literacy experiences before he started school, learning to read became difficult because he used only his personal knowledge to figure out what the text said. He made many miscues because he didn't know how to use letter sounds to check his expectation of what the word said. He continued to rely on his strength — personal knowledge — to try to figure out the word. When this didn't work, he made up the story by looking at the pictures. If this strategy is used occasionally, Sandy will continue to progress, but if he constantly uses his own knowledge without linking it to the words of the story, his reading will become hesitant and halting because nothing will fit.

Trish, on the other hand, learned phonics easily and, like some struggling readers, believed reading consisted of calling words precisely. She assumed that the meaning is found entirely in the print. When asked to demonstrate her comprehension, she answered the teacher's questions by repeating the words in the text. As stories became more complicated and teachers asked her to interpret the author's meaning rather than repeat the words, she began to struggle and had trouble making sense of these more elaborate stories. She could no longer indicate her understanding by repeating the words in the text; rather, she needed to combine what she already knew with the information in the text to interpret the author's meaning. If Trish continues to read stories without making sense, her reading will falter.

TEACHING APPROACH

For these readers, teachers start by using regular classroom materials or modifications to select instructional procedures that enable students to make sense of stories using what they already know and do. Later, they show these students how to link sources of information. In Sandy's case, for example, the following sequence builds on what he can already do to show him more appropriate strategies:

— To help develop his phonic awareness, Sandy reads several stories, primarily from predictable books with rhyming words.
— He rewrites one of the books, replacing characters and actions in the story with rhyming words. The teacher shows him words that rhyme with the targeted word.
— The teacher demonstrates a few rules of phonics by showing him how his knowledge of the rhyming words — a strength he has acquired — can help him decode unknown words by comparing them to known words. He might, for example, substitute initial consonants in rhyming words.

Children like Sandy and Trish need instruction that shows them how to link knowledge sources. Some special programs focus on identifying and correcting weaknesses rather than identifying and consciously supporting strengths. After identifying a weakness, these programs provide remedial drills that focus on skills in a context that is divorced from authentic literacy activities. Unfortunately, children who reach the required standard on the isolated skill assessments continue to read selections that are too hard for them, a situation that magnifies their difficulties. They cease to expand their knowledge or strategies because few of their literacy endeavors make sense.

Difficulty Elaborating Content and Strategy Knowledge

When children are continually expected to read demanding texts, they expend their energy constructing a hazy model of meaning. They are so occupied trying to make sense of the story that they do not expand their knowledge of the topic. As a result, they do not organize their strategies so that they can readily apply them in other literacy situations. Struggling readers are, in fact, often expected to read extremely difficult material and to complete workbook pages to reinforce reading skills at the expense of reading whole stories.

Proficient readers, who encounter few unfamiliar words, are expected to read extensively. In contrast, struggling readers read substantially less and miss about every third word. When this happens, the gap between what struggling readers know and what they are asked to read is so great that they cannot coordinate how they are reading or elaborate on their under-standing. Instead, they rely on what they can already do, making sense of text only infrequently.

For example, Sandy is so focused on using his previous knowledge to help decode the text that he is able to add no new information to the knowledge he already possesses. He avoids looking at the words on the page because they are difficult. Initially, he did try looking at the first letter and guessing. When this strategy stopped paying off, however, he gave up. Rather than linking information sources and figuring out how these sources can be integrated, he started relying exclusively on his own previous knowledge. This prevents him from developing flexible procedures for decoding unfamiliar words. His reading will become slower and less accurate until, finally, he will begin reading word by word.

TEACHING APPROACH

Struggling readers like Sandy and Trish need to read lots of authentic stories that are familiar enough for them to examine their trouble-shooting strategies. As students progress through literacy development, it becomes routine for them to make links between the words in the text and what they know about words. This enables them to use more of their thinking capacity to comprehend the topic, organize thoughtful responses and concentrate on explaining their strategies.

In essence, fluent reading enables students to clarify the links between the text and the strategies they use to make sense of the text. When struggling readers are continually subjected to literacy experiences where they cannot read fluently, they become oblivious to the strategies they use and are unable to integrate the meaning of new words that would, in turn, help them figure out unfamiliar words. They fail to develop an extensive network of information sources. For readers like Sandy and Trish, the links among knowledge sources have broken down. They rely exclusively on their strengths and fail to develop other strategies. And, because so little of what they read makes sense, they passively read words without expecting anything to make sense.

Difficulty Monitoring Meaning

When students rely on their strengths without expanding their understanding or the repertoire of strategies they can draw on, they grow accustomed to reading without making sense. This produces a muddled system for checking their responses.

Struggling readers appear to lack strategies that good readers use naturally. When queried, struggling readers glumly reply, "I don't know." And, in reality, they really don't know how to restore their understanding. They read the words and they know that what they read doesn't make sense, but they don't know how to change this situation. Because these readers have little experience constructing meaning, they passively read words without actively questioning their understanding. For example, when reading aloud, they seldom correct their mistakes, answering questions by repeating the words exactly as they appear in the text. When reading for understanding, they seldom revise their predictions, sticking with their initial predictions even when the text includes no evidence to support them.

For these readers, simply making the text easier or modifying a technique will not change their passive approach to making meaning. Even when specific strategies are demonstrated to them, struggling readers are not convinced the strategies will work or that they are an important part of reading. For example, Sandy and Trish knew they didn't understand, but they didn't know how to regain meaning because they had used their inappropriate alternative strategies for so long. They really don't know what strategies are or how to apply them.

TEACHING APPROACH

Sandy and Trish need to see examples of how to think when they encounter difficulty. For instance, Trish needs to learn to say to herself, This is not making sense. I can change how I'm reading. I need to reread the last paragraph and think about what I know. Even after seeing an example of how this strategy can work, she will need coaching as she begins to use it.

Likewise, teachers need to help struggling readers identify strategies and see the relationship between the strategies they use and their interpretation of the text. For instance, when Trish and Sandy interpret text successfully, they need to talk about the strategies they used to construct meaning and think about how effective these strategies were. Sharing interpretations with their peers helps them think about how they arrived at their answers by combining their own knowledge with the information in the text. During a discussion like this, they also help each other evaluate the strategies they used. Shared discussions help them learn that the strategies they use, rather than their ability, affects their understanding.

Unfortunately, remedial programs have been based on specific skill packets and workbooks where progress is monitored according to the number of right and wrong answers to questions. When reading is reduced to mastering a skill that readers lack, they increasingly define reading as a no-win situation. Their passive reading behavior becomes entrenched and they finally give up the whole miserable attempt.

Difficulty Interpreting the Situational Context

When students find themselves in literacy situations where they continually fail, they abandon their sense-making strategies and come to believe that they are doomed to failure. Struggling readers believe that they lack the ability to learn. They think to themselves, I will not try, because if I try and fail again, I am admitting I am dumb. Then, to preserve their sense of self-worth, they stop trying, thus eliminating the possibility of being dumb.

This attitude is perpetuated by the use of norm-referenced evaluations that reward students with above-average ability. For example, Sandy and Trish try hard, but they don't measure up to the standards set by students who learn easily and quickly. Soon they realize that their efforts will not guarantee success. So Sandy and Trish create excuses for not having their work completed, thereby avoiding a sense of failure and regaining their sense of self-worth by simply not trying. In fact, Sandy and Trish may never stay with a task long enough to discover that they can be successful.

This is the beginning of a vicious cycle. Because they don't appear to care about their own learning, their teacher decides they are lazy and unmotivated. But, Sandy and Trish are actually highly motivated — to preserve their sense of self-worth in the face of failure. What's more, because of their repeated failures, the two have developed a fuzzy notion about both success and failure. They attribute their failure to being stupid, a characteristic that cannot be changed, and they cease to expend effort. When they do succeed, on the other hand, they maintain that it was because of the easy materials or their teacher's effort rather than their own.

Because teachers have often focused on skills that students don't possess and asked them to complete drill exercises in a one-to-one situation isolated from any discussion about the meaning of stories, struggling readers develop a two-pronged definition of reading:

— Reading is getting the answers right.
— Reading is something "I can't do."

Measuring themselves by this definition, these struggling readers judge themselves to be poor readers, reducing their motivation.

TEACHING APPROACH

Sandy and Trish need to envision themselves as members of the literacy community. To help them do this, their teachers need to change the quality of the interactions within their classrooms. One way teachers can do this is by reviewing their own prompting behaviors. For instance, during oral reading, teachers often interrupt to give struggling readers a word as soon as they make an error, conveying the message that these children are incapable of making sense of the mistake on their own. If, on the other hand, teachers treat struggling readers the same way as successful students — by prompting them to think about what would make sense as they skip the word and read to the end of the sentence — they convey the message that the children are capable of figuring out the word themselves.

Teachers can also promote the idea that all students are members of a literacy community by reviewing their questioning strategies. In *Lively Discussions! Fostering Engaged Reading*, Janice Almasi points out that students often perceive that teachers want only right answers to questions. This impression is reinforced by the fact that teachers often direct complex questions only to the more successful students, either giving struggling readers the answer or excusing them from offering a response at all. Teachers can counter this impression by asking struggling readers more open-ended questions that require them to make inferences and judgments using the text and what they already know. As they ask the questions, teachers can also prompt struggling readers or give them hints, providing them with an opportunity to construct meaningful responses.

In addition, teachers can initiate more open-ended discussions in which everyone's response is valued. Struggling readers can participate in discussions, and teachers can name the strategies they use as they are talking. As teachers do this, they help struggling readers identify their use of a particular strategy within an authentic literacy discussion.

Teachers need to help struggling readers identify the strategies they use and understand that there is a relationship among the strategies they use, their interpretation of the text, and the effort they expend. For example, when Trish and Sandy are successful, they need to assess the strategies they used, as well as their effort. They need to be helped to define literacy as an active process that involves using the strategies they already possess.

Summary

The inability to read proficiently is not an innate, unchangeable characteristic. Teachers and schooling have a powerful influence on struggling readers, and the quality of classroom instruction has a direct effect on students' reading behaviors. This chapter examined four reasons students experience reading difficulties:

— Struggling readers often rely on a single information source, shifting away from using strategies that haven't been successful.
— They're often asked to read difficult texts, placing them in a situation where they cannot readily integrate new information with their strategies.
— They read and write passively because much of what they're asked to read doesn't make sense to them.

23

— Struggling readers who have failed repeatedly perceive the literacy event as a failure situation, thus decreasing their motivation.

. . . .

GUIDELINES

FOR INSTRUCTION

Because instruction can help or hinder literacy development, we, as teachers, must be mindful of the instructional choices we make as we respond to the needs of struggling readers. We must think about how our instruction affects the way students perceive the context, link information sources, develop strategies and check their understanding. In the context of what we know about the reasons children experience reading difficulties, this chapter suggests guidelines for teaching struggling readers.

Focus on What Children Can Do

Because struggling readers unconsciously shift away from a weakness and rely on what they can already do, sensitive teachers create literacy activities that encourage them to build on the successful strategies they already possess. For example, teachers can use a variety of prompts to encourage readers to use their natural abilities. One teacher was working with a child who could sound out words, but using this strategy alone caused him to read slowly and impaired his comprehension. As he stumbled over an unfamiliar word in a passage he was reading aloud, the teacher began by asking, "What would make sense and sounds like what you're saying?" This prompt, which encouraged him to think about what made sense in the context of the passage, enabled him to use his facility in sounding out words.

As well as encouraging students to use their strengths to solve difficulties, but they also ask them to use this strength in combination with other strategies. When teachers use instructional techniques that encourage children to demonstrate what they can already do, this positive experience motivates them to engage in reading and writing activities. Then, as they add more complex strategies to those they already possess, teachers help them expand the repertoire of strategies they can draw on.

Focus on Making Sense

Many struggling readers become so involved in decoding individual words that they forget to try to make sense out of an entire sentence or passage. Fortunately, from a very young age, children strive to make sense of their world — and sensitive teachers build on this natural curiosity by supporting them in making sense of reading and writing activities. In their search for meaning, developing readers invent their own explanations and justify these with increasingly elaborate explanations.

The language of teaching can often encourage a "making sense" perspective. Even a teacher's non-verbal behavior can empower students to make sense of text. One teacher of six- and seven-year-olds, for example, simply scratches her head in wonderment when something a student says doesn't make sense. Some teachers use questions like, "Did that make sense?" Others combine prompts, always from the perspective that the words must make sense: "What makes sense and begins with the letter F?"

During a discussion of a story, the line of questioning can communicate the expectation that the words will make sense. If teachers ask a string of unrelated questions aimed at eliciting only facts, students develop the idea that the purpose of reading is to get the facts right rather than construct meaningful responses. Sensitive teachers prepare discussion questions that will lead struggling readers to construct a cohesive view of the story. In all their instruction, these teachers build on the students' natural inclination to make sense of the world.

Use Familiar Topics

Because struggling readers encounter many experiences that are too challenging for them, teachers must ensure that they are asked to read material within their reading level that is familiar enough for them to employ sense-making strategies. These stories need to be read with no more than one error every 10 words, a 90 per cent accuracy rate. At this rate, children are able to make sense of the text and activate fix-up strategies. If they make more than one error every 10 words, they can't understand enough to correct their mistakes.

When choosing material, the teacher considers the students' reading proficiency and the extent of their previous experiences with the topic. Along with the students, she chooses stories that are familiar enough that the children can readily predict, monitor and expand on the content of the passage. Additionally, she carefully selects authentic texts so the children can identify with the main character's conflict and successfully predict solutions based on their own experiences. Likewise, she encourages students to write about their own experiences using familiar language. In this way, they generate longer and more well-formed texts. The more students read and write about familiar topics, the greater their understanding.

Ask Children What They Already Know

Even when struggling readers know a great deal about a subject, they often forget to use this knowledge as they read, acting as if answers will magically emerge from school books. Because school-related tasks often seem unrelated to real life, they tend leave their previous knowledge at home. But reading and writing about what you know is critical to engaging actively in literacy activities.

Sensitive teachers ask students what they know about topics and help them actively use this information as they read. For example, a 12-year-old boy read a story about a young girl whose father always let her have her way. In interpreting the story, he could not predict what would happen even though his experience in his own family, where his sister always got her way, was similar. When the teacher asked him about the interactions in his home and if there were any similarities between them and the story, he was slowly able to begin to use his own experience to interpret the actions of the main character.

Struggling readers often need help figuring out when and how to use what they already know. As they lead discussions about stories, sensitive teachers think about each child's experiences and how these can be used.

Discuss Stories with Peers

Struggling readers often receive extensive skills instruction in isolated situations in which their only interaction is with the teacher about the correctness of their responses. Situations like this inhibit the development of a sense of story and how language works. Developing readers benefit from situations in which they read and write about complete stories because doing so helps them internalize how written language and stories work. When they understand the structure of printed language, they have less difficulty shifting between what they already know and the text, which helps them interpret stories.

Not only do students need to read whole stories, but they also need to discuss them. During discussions, students share their interpretations, focus their purposes and think about the functions of reading and writing. They discuss how they constructed their responses, justifying their interpretations based on the story and on what they already know. Thus, readers need experiences where they can discuss their thinking about a topic in both small and large groups.

Revisit Text

Struggling readers have difficulty expanding their knowledge of content and of the strategies they use. Revisiting texts helps them do both. When they reread a passage, the structure of the text and the topic are already familiar, so they can make connections between what they already know and the information presented in the text. This allows for a deeper processing of the information. Not only can they expand their knowledge of the topic, but they can also think about how they are constructing their interpretation. Research indicates that rereading increases fluent, strategic reading, which helps students use more effective trouble-shooting strategies by giving them time to think.

Reading with a partner is one effective technique for encouraging children to reread a selection. For example, two children might reread a passage, using their own words to tell the other about a favorite part.

Another technique involves creating a play script and inviting small groups to read aloud each part. This helps struggling readers participate in classroom activities with their peers.

Teachers must look for opportunities to create authentic activities for revisiting text, which enables struggling readers to expand their knowledge of both the topic and their strategies.

Coach Literate Behaviors

Because struggling readers have continually experienced reading without making sense, they are often unaware of when and how to use strategies as they read and write. Sensitive teachers act as coaches by observing the strategies students already use, then explaining and demonstrating thinking that will augment these strategies. In these instances, the teacher thinks aloud about how he would remedy a particular difficulty. For example, when one child continued to answer questions using only information from the text, the teacher began to recall the textual information himself, then demonstrated how he thought about this information in light of his own previous knowledge. He then asked the child to relate similar experiences and construct a response.

This coaching in how to think involves demonstrating procedures for removing difficulties in making interpretations. To do this, the teacher purposely makes mistakes while reading so he can demonstrate how he monitors his own active search for meaning. Too often, struggling readers perceive literacy as error-free reading and correct writing. By making mistakes, the teacher shows students his own coping behaviors and demonstrates that mistakes can be valuable learning tools rather than indications of failure.

This demonstration and the subsequent coaching helps struggling readers develop a risk-taking attitude toward literacy events. As students talk about how they solve problems, the teacher has an opportunity to provide support and feed-back about their thinking. He provides encouragement by commenting on their trouble-shooting behavior, possibly saying something like: "I noticed the way you used your knowledge about Africa to figure out that the country was Egypt."

When coaching this way, the teacher phases in to support effective strategies and phases out to allow children to think independently, gradually increasing the time he waits before offering support so that the children have time to develop their own responses. When offering support, the teacher probes the children's reasoning by using parts of their answers to demonstrate thinking.

Give Children Choice

Engaging struggling readers in structured learning activities can be tricky. Because they have experienced failure, whether in the short or long term, they are often extremely skeptical of any activity that a *teacher* might suggest. Giving students the opportunity to choose among selected options can increase their level of engagement in an activity and the degree of enthusiasm they bring to reading.

Teachers can engage children in defining what they want to know in several ways. Students can, for example, select the topic or the reading material, a process that helps them begin to define their own reasons for reading. Many teachers also use literature circles or thematic units that allow students to choose what they will read and write. Some teachers ask students to choose how they will read and respond to the readings — alone, with a partner or in a group. Other teachers set up student-led discussion groups and circulate among the groups. In their groups, the students not only choose the books they will read, but they also decide how much they will read each day and what they will discuss. Janice Almasi found that student-led discussions helped children clarify misunderstandings that would not have even been discussed in traditional reading groups.

In other classrooms, students are invited to choose how they will respond to a reading. Working in small groups or pairs, they may write a report, perform a play, make a video or conduct interviews. In each case, the students use their responses to demonstrate their understanding of the reading selection.

Ask Children What They Learned

Because they continually experience failure, struggling readers develop a hazy idea of both their successes and failures. Teachers can help these students develop a realistic assessment of their literate behavior by asking them to describe how they think and read. This self-assessment helps them recognize their successes as well as the strategies they use. The teacher then discusses the relationship among their effort, their use of various strategies, and their successful interpretations of the text.

These discussions can be supported in several ways. For example, inviting children to choose what to include in their assessment portfolio can help them evaluate their performance and show them that they have made progress over time. Deciding what represents their best work requires students to define reading and writing behaviors, and asking them to reflect on why a particular piece was selected helps them describe their literacy. For instance, one struggling 10-year-old said, "I chose this story map because I liked doing story maps. Story maps helped me think about why the character did that." Although this is just a beginning, articulating why a particular piece was selected helps students evaluate what is involved in reading and what they do well during reading.

Students can also evaluate their performance at various literacy activities. For instance, one group of seven- and eight-year-old struggling readers retold a story they had read as the teacher recorded their summary. When they were finished, the teacher made copies of the summary, then gave everyone a checksheet like the one on the following page to help them evaluate the summary. Using the checksheet, the students and teacher assessed the summary together, deciding whether it included the main characters, setting, problem, major events and the resolution of the problem.

When they had finished filling in the checksheet, the children revised the summary, adding more detail about some aspects of the story and cutting the amount of detail about others. The teacher made new copies, and this became their reading material.

Story Summary Checksheet

	Yes	Oops!
Setting		
Did I begin the story with an introduction?	❑	❑
Did I include statements about time and place?	❑	❑
Did I include other characters?	❑	❑
Problem		
Did I tell about the main character's problems?	❑	❑
Did I tell about several key events?	❑	❑
Resolution		
Did I tell how the problem was solved?	❑	❑
Did I put an ending on the story?	❑	❑

Students can also discuss the strategies they use and the effort expended. One teacher created a chart like the following. After reading a story, students use the chart to rate their predictions, assessing the relationship between effort and strategy use. After evaluating the process she used to make predictions, one student wrote: "I am predicting more and more. Now I need to check my predictions with what's in the story."

Today's Evaluation

1 = Not Good 2 = Okay 3 = Good 4 = Very Good

I made predictions.	1 2 3 4
Most of my predictions used only what I knew.	1 2 3 4
Most of my predictions used only what the text said.	1 2 3 4
Most of my predictions used both what the text said and what I knew.	1 2 3 4

Summary of Strategies and Comprehension

_____

_____

Assessments like these help struggling readers attribute their performance to their own previous knowledge or skill at using strategies rather than to luck, the easiness of materials or their innate abilities. They also identify key aspects of various strategies and the effects of using them. Strategy use is a flexible measure that changes with various tasks, while ability is a relative stable measure. Asking readers what they learned engages them in evaluating their success or failure on the basis of the strategies they used and identifies strategies that they are able to change.

Support Children's Membership in the Literacy Community

Struggling readers are often uncomfortable with literacy activities because they view literacy as something they don't possess. As Frank Smith says in his book, *Joining the Literacy Club*, sensitive teachers ensure that all children view themselves as members of the literacy community by inviting children to participate in collaborative and meaningful literacy activities. Time is set aside each day for personal reading and writing when students can read books they have selected themselves for their own purposes and write about their own ideas. These teachers also set aside time to share ideas the children have gained from personal reading and writing.

When doing this, teachers and students share their own interpretations and queries, creating an environment in which everyone takes risks while constructing meaning. It is also important for teachers to share their own personal responses as readers and writers so that they, too, are viewed as members of the literacy community.

Summary

Using these guidelines, teachers can build an effective instructional program that supports struggling readers as they make sense of text. By using familiar topics to build on what children can already do, teachers ensure that the children experience success. Asking children what they want to learn as well as what they already know involves them in the literacy activities. Likewise, discussing whole stories with their peers enables children to share their interpretations and discuss reading strategies in a situation in which the activities make sense. As children revisit text and benefit from the teacher's coaching, they extend their troubleshooting behaviors and begin to take more risks. And, as teachers ask children what they learned and include them in the literacy community, students begin to view themselves as readers and writers.

. . . .

LITERACY DEVELOPMENT—

A CONTINUING PROCESS

We all pass through a series of phases as we develop physically. For instance, we learn to crawl before we walk and we learn to walk before we run. As children grow and mature, they also progress through phases of literacy development, learning first to talk, then to read and write. Although specific characteristics are certainly associated with each phase, the five stages of literacy development — emergent, grounded, expanding, strategic and reflective — are not separate from each other, nor are their boundaries sharply defined. Rather, they overlap, as each grows out of the previous phase. The diagram on the following page illustrates this overlap.

As developing readers encounter more difficult passages, they use the active learning process to develop new generalizations about literacy. As they meet the challenge of each new phase of literacy, they augment their repertoire of literacy strategies. Thus, as they make the transition from one phase to the next, critical learning occurs and this enhances future literacy development. In the transitional stages, students not only encounter the new challenge presented by more difficult text, but they also refine and weave together the knowledge they gained during the previous phase, fitting the resulting insights into their personal literacy framework. During this time, the challenges encountered lead to new thinking and increase the interconnections among literacy behaviors.

This chapter provides an overview of the five phases of literacy development and suggests teaching strategies that can be used during each phase. Both the phases and teaching strategies are discussed in greater detail in subsequent chapters. Because literacy development flows along a continuum, it's worth remembering that none of the teaching strategies need be restricted to a particular phase. Rather, instruction needs to focus on individual readers and *their* development.

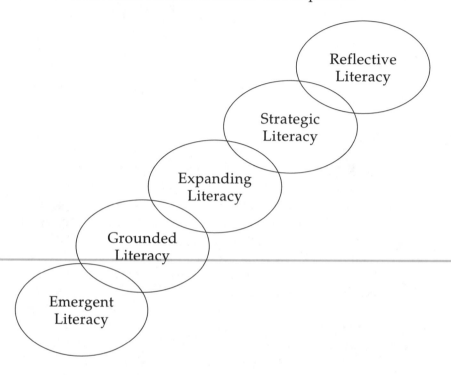

Emergent Literacy

During the emergent literacy phase, children become aware of the symbols in their environment, learning, for example, that the golden arches represent McDonald's. This kind of recognition — that a symbol represents a familiar concept — marks the the early beginning of print awareness. As parents read and re-read stories to them, children begin to associate the symbols on the printed page with the words their parents are saying and, indeed, often memorize their favorite books. When they write their names, they learn that the pattern of letters in words is consistent. As they integrate these experiences, young readers use their knowledge of the social context, such as memorizing stories with Mom and Dad, to figure out how print works. This phase is often referred to as emerging literacy because the literacy behaviors seem to emerge naturally out of the children's experiences — without formal instruction.

At school, teachers try to emulate these early experiences by creating situations that help developing readers make associations between what is said and what is written. For example, when using the language experience approach, a teacher might create a shared experience like collecting leaves on a walk. This situates the literacy event that follows. As the teacher records the children's description of the walk on an experience chart, it represents an authentic situation. The children see their spoken language written down and use their understanding of the situation to figure out the words in the story. This situated literacy development continues until these readers begin to meet new challenges.

Grounded Literacy

As developing readers begin to encounter unfamiliar words and longer stories, they develop new strategies to meet this challenge. As their literacy development becomes grounded in textual conventions, their comprehension relies less on understanding the social context and using the illustrations in picture books. For example, when they double-check the text to verify their understanding, they must examine the print, looking closely at the patterns of letters and words. To figure out unfamiliar words in new stories, they might ask themselves, What makes sense and looks like this word? or What word do I know that has the same letter patterns? When they do this, they are using decoding analogies. In other words, they are visualizing words they know and matching the letter patterns and sounds to the new word. Thus, developing readers begin to rely on textual patterns to help confirm their predictions.

As their literacy activities shift from predominantly oral shared reading to silent reading and discussion, youngsters are asked to reflect their overall understanding of the story by discussing what they read. These activities require developing readers to ground their literacy in the textual conventions of story grammar. When they retell stories, they use the story pattern (i.e., main character, problem, specific events and resolution) to provide a framework for their retelling and discussion. Thus, the textual patterns help readers make predictions and revise their understanding.

To help focus developing readers' attention on the structure of the text and ground their literacy in the conventions of the text, teachers can help students look for patterns in words and stories. Framed rhyming innovations is a teaching approach that helps children focus on these patterns by rewriting favorite rhyming stories. "I was walking down the road / Then I saw a little toad," for example, might be rewritten as "I was sitting on a mat / Then I saw a little cat." As the children figure out words to replace the key rhyming words, they must focus on what makes sense and fits into the story. As they match letter patterns to known words, they must think about the letters in words, as well as about how the story is formed and whether the new story pattern makes sense. This focus on textual conventions continues until these readers begin to meet new challenges.

Expanding Literacy

As they progress through the first two phases of literacy, readers develop extensive knowledge of the conventions of print, both in words and in stories. As developing readers ground their literacy in textual conventions, however, they lose fluency. As they enter the expanding literacy phase, their focus shifts from developing this knowledge to using it as they read. Therefore, the challenge of the expanding literacy phase is to broaden children's literacy to help equip them to associate their knowledge of both print and a particular topic with what is written on the page. This involves linking sources concurrently so that their fluency in word identification integrates with their fluency in developing ideas.

During the expanding literacy phase, instruction focuses on fluent reading by making sense of sentences. Students learn that groups of words — phrases, clauses and sentences — make meaning and that sentences have predictable structures that influence meaning. Their oral reading is marked by a growing smoothness that is represented by appropriate phrasing, expression and pauses to communicate a message.

During the expanding literacy phase, teachers often invite children to reread text and predict meaning in various ways. The purpose is to focus students' attention on connecting meaning and words simultaneously. This helps them construct meaning by predicting what phrases or other chunks of language will say. In this way, developing readers are encouraged to think about how the context of a sentence influences meaning, word identification and fluency. This characteristic of predicting sentence meaning continues until these readers begin to meet new challenges.

Strategic Literacy

As students become adept at applying familiar strategies, they face a new challenge. During the strategic literacy phase, they assert new control over their thinking as they begin experimenting with ways of thinking about the process they use to construct meaning. This new phase of "thinking about thinking" enables them to take control of their comprehension and plan the probable outcomes of procedures related to how they construct an answer. As they take control of their strategies for learning, they interpret things from a personal point of view, which enables them to experiment with their ideas about the world.

TEACHING APPROACH

During the strategic literacy phase, teachers can focus students' attention on personal reading strategies and interpretations. They choose techniques that ask students to construct personal meaning and analyze how they constructed it, differentiating their own knowledge from the author's meaning. To create their responses, students learn to think about their ideas and separate them from those of the author. These activities help developing readers take control of their personal literacy strategies and interpretations. This personal fascination with their own literacy development continues until these readers begin to meet new challenges.

Reflective Literacy

The final challenge of developing readers is to use reading and writing as tools to construct and communicate meaning. In the reflective literacy phase, they begin to look beyond their own point of view and recognize that others exist. During this phase of literacy, students select critical information from various sources to extend their own point of view. Using this information, they justify their point of view and distinguish it from that of others. Further, they support their position by summarizing information from various literary sources. They synthesize critical information and organize it in order to remember and communicate it. Finally, they communicate their thinking by using an expressive form appropriate to the situation. They might, for example, participate in a debate, make a video or write a term paper. In other words, they translate the understanding gained through reading into various media.

TEACHING APPROACH

During the reflective literacy phase, teachers use techniques to focus readers' attention on thinking about what is important to remember and justifying their point of view. These techniques ask children to use their personal understanding to organize textual information. Developing readers learn to justify their selection of important concepts and explain how they synthesized the information and communicated their ideas in various forms.

Summary

Literacy development occurs in overlapping phases that flow along a continuum. Moving through the five phases — emergent literacy, grounded literacy, expanding literacy, strategic literacy and reflective literacy — can take a lifetime. Understanding the challenges of each phase increases the likelihood that teachers can not only help struggling readers meet the current challenge, but also guide them into even more challenging activities.

The chapters that follow provide more detailed information about each phase, pinpoint difficulties readers might encounter, and suggest instructional strategies to help overcome these. These strategies need not be limited to a particular phase but may be used during all phases of development for very different reasons. Sensitive teachers analyze each teaching technique to evaluate how it can be used to advance a reader's development.

. . . .

EMERGENT LITERACY

During the emergent literacy phase, readers combine what they already know with the situational context to predict — and check — the meaning of printed symbols. As they do so, they acquire knowledge about written language. They use this information to figure out what the words on the page say.

Difficulties

When developing readers use only what they can already do to help them decode text, they run into trouble. Some rely too much on their own knowledge, without matching what they say to what the text on the page says. They seem to know so much that they are unconcerned with printed words. Others run into difficulty because they rely only on the situation to help them. This may, for example, involve listening to the rhythm and intonation of stories read aloud without matching what they hear to the words on the page. When they make miscues, they look to the teacher, rather than the text, to supply the correct word. In doing so, they are relying exclusively on the context rather than developing a variety of strategies for identifying words.

Other struggling readers simply don't have enough background knowledge to make sense of the text. They repeat what the teacher says without understanding what they are reading and often end up reading word by word, hoping against hope that something will make sense.

Instructional Strategies

The following instructional strategies emphasize building on the children's strengths to help them move towards literate behaviors. The strategies that will be discussed are the language experience approach, using predictable books in a shared reading setting, using talking books, using familiar books, buddy reading and the thematic approach, as well how to use reading recovery and other similar programs. Though these are suggestions for meeting the needs of struggling readers during this phase, they may be used during other phases for very different reasons. Sensitive teachers evaluate how a particular technique can improve the literacy of each child.

LANGUAGE EXPERIENCE

Some developing readers rely exclusively on their previous knowledge of a topic to help them decode text. To build on this background knowledge and their natural ability to use oral language to communicate, teachers invite these students to dictate stories about everyday experiences. The teacher records the story on a large piece of paper and, when it is finished, reads it with the child to check content.

Then, teacher and child read the story several times together, providing the youngster with an opportunity to connect her background knowledge with the printed words. Each child then reads the story on her own and draws a picture to accompany it. In this way, the story becomes the instructional text and a collection of stories can become a reader.

There is a danger that some children will rapidly memorize the story they dictate and continue to focus on the social aspects of the literacy event rather than looking closely at the text. When this happens, teachers can copy chunks of the story onto cards and ask the children to read these in the order they appeared in the story. If they have trouble recognizing a word or phrase, the teacher prompts by asking questions like, "What did you say in the story after ...?" or "You said, `(repeats the preceding section),' and then what did you say in the story?" These cues focus on making the shift between oral and printed language. By building on their natural strengths, this approach helps struggling readers decode the printed words.

Some developing readers become so involved in the social context that they fail to look at the text. They might, for example, dictate elaborate stories to the teacher, then be unable to read what they said. For these — and other developing readers — using predictable books in a shared reading setting facilitates their fluency as well as their ability to identify words.

The teacher and children choose a predictable book, often a big book, that has a rhythmic, repetitive language pattern. Together, they read the book, with the teacher taking the lead during the first reading.

The teacher and children read the book several more times. During the second and third readings, the teacher begins to leave out words that can be predicted from the language pattern. For example, "I can hug my sister. I can hug my. ..." Using their sense of language patterns, the children supply the missing word (in this case, "brother"). Eventually, they take over the reading of the story from the teacher.

Afterwards, the children read the book on their own. The teacher can phase in at any time to assist if they stumble over the language pattern.

When reading predictable books, children use their knowledge of the topic, story structure and language patterns to predict what the text will say. When they make a miscue, the teacher offers prompts like: "Remember the pattern ... and look at the picture. Now what would this phrase say?" Or he may simply prompt with: "This phrase is about a dog. How would the pattern go?" This helps struggling readers use their sense of the patterns of language to figure out unfamiliar words.

THEMATIC APPROACH

Some developing readers have only limited experiences of the world and of using language to draw on. In many cases, the experience they do possess is difficult to connect to the stories that are used in school. Because they don't readily use language, their language experience stories are not well developed.

Teachers can create literacy activities around extended themes to bolster the language and experiential resources of these children. This approach helps them construct a network of knowledge related to a particular topic. Children can draw on this knowledge when reading.

Once the theme is selected, the teacher needs to collect a variety of related reading material. She reads this aloud to the children, querying them about and discussing what they've learned.

After reading several books on the topic, the teacher and students work together to generate lists of what they've learned. These can be used to create a book or report about the theme, which can then become their reading text.

The children and teacher continue in this fashion, creating books about topics that are similar to the original theme. For instance, a group of young Aboriginal students lacked the knowledge of English necessary to read stories in predictable books or create their own stories. Their teacher read aloud several books about a buffalo hunt, showed pictures of a hunt and encouraged the children to talk about hunting buffalo. The children then created a book about buffalo hunting. Then they read and wrote stories about hunting deer. Finally, they read and wrote about a lion hunt in Africa.

In their theme books, the children used the same basic vocabulary, developing a background of experiences with both the content and print. If they were unable to identify a word, the teacher asked them to think about the other stories they had read to help figure it out. This encouraged them to build a network of meaning that they could draw on to help them identify words and expand their knowledge of the topic.

TALKING BOOKS

Some developing readers need to hear a story repeatedly so they can remember both the words and the sequence of events. Talking books, which are prerecorded readings of selected stories, help young readers associate what they hear with the text by providing them with the opportunity to hear and read a story many times.

The teacher and child select a book and tape that are interesting and short enough to complete in a single session. The child listens to and reads along with the tape until he can read the story fluently on his own. Once he can do so, he reads it orally to the teacher, who evaluates his oral reading, fluency and comprehension.

As they listen to and read talking books, children memorize the story and use this experience to anticipate what the words will be. Their familiarity with the story enables them to attend to both the meaning and the print at the same time. If they have difficulty, the teacher can read aloud the passage so they can hear the intonation and relate it to the message. The teacher also encourages them to listen to the story again, paying particular attention to the difficult sections.

This technique enables struggling readers to use the overall meaning of the story to figure out unknown words and frees the teacher to work with other children while those experiencing difficulty are listening to the tape.

FAMILIAR BOOKS AND BUDDY READING

Familiar stories are selections children have already read and know well. Most teachers have a classroom library full of predictable books, easy readers and language experience stories that the children have already read. These familiar materials offer a comfortable reading experience that encourages beginning readers to practice the strategies they are developing. Reading these familiar stories aloud to a reading buddy increases the amount of reading children do each day, offering them an opportunity to practice reading and focus on features of print and meaning. When children encounter words within the familiar context of a well-known story, they are able to read them more easily, which boosts their confidence. The experience is both fun and satisfying because they are learning new ways to figure out print and meaning.

READING RECOVERY

Reading recovery is actually an intervention program rather than an instructional technique. However, it has proven extremely effective with six- and seven-year-old struggling readers who receive an individual 30-minute lesson every day in addition to regular classroom instruction.

In *The Early Detection of Reading Difficulties*, Marie Clay suggests that each session start with a reading of a familiar story. This encourages fluent, rhythmic reading that helps the child both experience what it feels like to read expressively and develop her reading strategies.

A new book, selected because the language structures in the text match the child's, is then introduced. The teacher and child review and discuss the story, paying particular attention to the story line. The teacher explains unfamiliar concepts using the language structure of the text, thus increasing the likelihood that the child will be able to read successfully on her own. As the child reads the story, the teacher assists as necessary, using as many meaning-focused prompts as possible.

Afterwards, the child writes a one- or two-sentence message. As the child writes, she stretches out the sounds in each word and matches letters and sounds. When she finishes creating the message, the teacher works with her to review the misspellings (see "Message Writing" in the next chapter).

After this, the teacher cuts apart the words and invites the child to reassemble the sentence. This aspect of the lesson begins by using the social context to construct a sentence and stretch out the sounds in words as the teacher scaffolds the child's learning. It ends with the child independently manipulating single words to develop the concept of word and letter.

Throughout the sessions, the teacher monitors the development of the child's reading strategies by asking her to read a book that has been read only once before. As the child reads, the teacher records her miscues. This information is used to guide the prompting behavior the teacher uses during the instructional session as well as to measure the child's progress towards proficient reading.

BEYOND READING RECOVERY

The recent focus on beginning reading has led to the development of a range of intensive interventions designed to help children in their first year of schooling. Some require teachers to take extensive in-service training, while others require the school reading coordinator to provide continuing training. In addition, the reading recovery format has provided the developmental foundation for several programs that use leveled predictable materials. Some of these come with training videotapes. James King who has spearheaded one program in Florida, reports that it is as effective as reading recovery, while

47

the videotapes reduce the need for school districts to organize extensive in-service programs.

In Montana, Rosie Battleson and I, along with a number of reading specialists, have developed the wish-plus program, which provides one-to-one tutoring on a withdrawal basis for six- to eight-year-olds who are at risk of failing to learn to read.

Each Wish-plus session begins with an interactive writing activity, in which the child writes a sentence of a continuing story. A more detailed description of interactive writing is included in the following chapter. After the sentence is written on a card strip and the words are cut apart, the children take the cards home and, with family members, practice putting the sentence together. The next day, the child returns the cards to the teacher, who glues the sentence on to colorful butcher paper.

On each of the next four or five days, the child adds another sentence to the story and reads what has been written to date. When the story is complete, the child takes the butcher paper to the regular classroom and reads the story to classmates before taking it home. At home, parents are encouraged to post the story in a prominent place and read it over and over with the child.

The rest of the wish-plus session may involve reading a familiar story, reading a new book, or reading aloud part of a story introduced the previous day to assess progress. When reading new books, the shared reading approach is used. Once the book has been read, the focus is on comprehension as children are asked to retell the story.

Some programs have adapted reading recovery procedures for use with small groups of children. The children in the group become powerful supports during the reading of predictable books and learn to offer prompts that increase the independent thinking of the other students.

In an article in *The Reading Teacher*, Barbara Taylor, Ruth Short, Barbara Frye and Brenda Shearer described an early intervention technique that reduces the number of unfamiliar words struggling readers must deal with. The sessions start with a whole-class reading of a big book. Over several days, a small group of struggling readers then works with the teacher to dictate a summary of the story, which the teacher records. The teacher supports the children by asking questions and offering hints about what comes next and so on. Every day, a sentence is added until the summary is complete. The children then use the summary as their reading material and, with the help of a teacher's aide or volunteer, repeat this reading until they are fluent.

As each sentence is added to the summary, the teacher stops at four or five words and demonstrates how to divide these into sounds and how to blend the sounds. On a sheet of paper, the teacher then draws a series of boxes that represent each of the sounds in each of the session's highlighted words. These papers are photocopied and handed out to individual students the next day. As the teacher says the words slowly, the children write the letter(s) that represents each sound in the appropriate box.

COMPUTER PROGRAMS

Several publishing companies now offer predictable books on CD-ROM. In most cases, a narrator reads aloud the story, highlighting the words on screen as they are read. As the children listen, they focus on the highlighted words on the screen, increasing their ability to identify words. Programs such as these offer the same kind of supported reading as shared reading experiences and talking books, while enabling the child to control the speed and repetition of the story.

Many of these programs also incorporate cloze activities that ask the child to fill in deleted words. This helps them learn to figure out new words by examining the context and promotes independence in reading. Some programs also enable the children to rewrite the predictable book by supplying words that fit in the context of the original story. Again this helps focus on letter-sound patterns in words.

Summary

The teaching strategies suggested in this chapter are examples of practices that have been successfully used with struggling readers during the emergent phase of literacy. Most of the strategies focus on showing these readers how to move beyond relying on the social context of literacy so that they can begin decoding the words themselves.

. . . .

GROUNDED LITERACY

When children in the emergent phase of literacy start using what they already know to help decode text, they are beginning to ground their literacy in the text itself, which prepares them to enter the next phase. In the grounded literacy phase, they use their sense of oral language to discover the patterns in written language. As they encounter more and more unfamiliar text while reading, they need strategies to help them figure out the words. At the same time, they must also develop their knowledge of how stories work. During the grounded literacy phase, literacy activities shift from predominantly oral, shared reading to silent reading and discussion. This shift means that students must be able to discuss what they read, drawing on their understanding of the plot and sequence of events in a story. It also requires developing readers to ground their literacy in textual conventions so that more fluent reading and thinking can develop.

Difficulties

During this phase, developing readers may experience difficulty because they have weaknesses that inhibit the natural evolution of their decoding strategies. Some readers, who have difficulty unlocking the patterns of sounds in words, continue using only their background knowledge, which fails them as they encounter unfamiliar passages more and more often.

Others have difficulty following the story line, which means they have trouble when asked to predict what might happen next or to discuss what they read. They can read the words on the page, but do not use these to construct meaning as they are reading.

Instructional Strategies

Instructional activities for children in the grounded literacy phase are directed towards processing both print and meaning. This processing focuses on the structure of text as readers ground their literacy in textual conventions.

To develop a sense of the code, developing readers must write, write, write. Although direct instruction in decoding will help them understand the code, writing helps their knowledge of written conventions to evolve naturally. As students write, they develop an understanding that groups of letters form words and that these groups follow patterns.

Message writing, framed rhyming innovations and interactive writing are techniques that highlight this decoding within a meaningful context. Both writing and repeated reading help children shift their attention to the words in the text and focus attention on the structure of the stories.

As developing readers shift from oral to silent reading, they need to understand the framework of a story. This knowledge helps them predict what the author will say next and retell the story. Instructional strategies that encourage children to retell stories and create story frames and character maps help them develop a sense of text structure when reading. The following techniques have been used effectively with struggling readers during this phase of literacy development.

MESSAGE WRITING

Some struggling readers, who begin to read by making up the text to fit pictures, become so involved in predicting meaning this way that they fail to check the words on the page. Message writing can help them focus on the letters in words.

The teacher provides a blank writing book in which the pages are divided in half, the top half for practice and the bottom for the message. The child thinks up a one- or two-sentence message and writes it by slowly saying the words in order to predict the letters they include. If he doesn't know the printed form of a word, he goes to the practice section of the page and the teacher assists by drawing a box for each letter. The child slowly voices the sounds and places the letters he knows in the appropriate boxes. Then the teacher prints the unknown letters where they belong and the child copies the new word into the message. When finished, he reads the entire message.

As children predict letters in words, they attend to the pattern of the letters, a strategy that transfers to reading stories. When they make a miscue, the teacher asks them to notice the letters and the word length as well as the overall textual meaning. The teacher also draws comparisons with words the children have already written in the messages. In this way, children develop their sense of the pattern of letters in words.

WORD SORTS

Rather than focusing on the sounds of individual letters, some struggling readers benefit from learning the patterns of letters in words. They readily notice patterns and use their knowledge of word patterns to figure out the sounds of letters. As a result, they are more successful when they are asked to focus on letter patterns rather than letter sounds.

Word sorts involve challenging children to group words printed on cards according to various patterns, then asking them to explain how they decided which category particular words belong in. For example, the teacher might show students three words that rhyme, such as "mat," "hat" and "rat." Then she asks, "Why do you think these words go together?" This focuses the students' attention on the letter patterns that are similar. The students then search their word bank to find other rhyming words that contain the same pattern.

WORD PROBES

Some struggling readers have great difficulty understanding decoding analogies. Because they do not readily notice the patterns of letters in similar words, these patterns must be highlighted for them. In an article that appeared in *The Reading Teacher*, Irene Gaskins and her colleagues suggest that a "word detective" program can help direct students' attention to these patterns. This involves posting a wall chart containing words that illustrate common English spelling patterns and teaching students how to use these key words to figure out unfamiliar words.

To begin, the teacher and students discuss various strategies for figuring out words. These might include using the meaning of the sentence along with the first letter of the word or using a word's sound patterns. Then the teacher selects a key word from the wall chart and says it slowly, stretching out all the sounds so that they can be heard clearly. As the students hear a sound, they hold up a finger. Then, they look at the word, matching the letters to the sounds they hear.

The teacher shows the children how to talk aloud about the word and its sound patterns by saying, "I hear X letters and I see Y letters because...." This helps them match the letters to the sounds they hear. Then the children name the spelling pattern, such as the "an" in the word "can." They create a list of other words that have the same spelling pattern (e.g., "man" and "plan"), as well as the same vowel sound (e.g., "cat" and "cap"). After this, the students read texts that contain words with similar spelling patterns.

INTERACTIVE WRITING

The roots of interactive writing can be traced to the language experience approach, which involves children in dictating a story to the teacher, and to shared writing, which involves children and teacher in writing a collaborative story. Interactive writing differs from these two approaches, however, because the children themselves do the writing. As they do so, the teacher's role is to help scaffold their thinking about the letters and sounds in words and about language conventions. Because of this, an interactive writing lesson provides many opportunities for direct teaching in a meaningful context.

In their book, *Guided Reading: Good First Teaching for All Children*, Irene Fountas and Gay Su Pinnell describe an interactive writing lesson. The children and teacher decide on a topic to write about, usually one that is tied to a classroom event or activity. The teacher then asks the children how to begin and they suggest an opening sentence. Together, teacher and children say the first word of this sentence slowly, then decide what letter represents the first sound they hear. The teacher asks a child to write that letter on a chart or the chalkboard.

Then, they say the word again and discuss what sound comes next. The teacher asks another child to add the letter that represents this sound.

Once the first word is written, teacher and children move on to the second word, continuing this way until the sentence is complete. The teacher's prompts are very important because they help scaffold the children's thinking about the words. Prompts may include questions like:

— Say the word slowly. What sounds do you hear?
— Can you write the letter that stands for that sound?
— Can you find the letter that we need to write on our alphabet chart?
— Would you point to and read what we have written so far?
— Would that make sense?
— Does that look right?

FRAMED RHYMING INNOVATIONS

Some struggling readers focus primarily on decoding isolated words without thinking about what makes sense in sentences and stories. Framed rhyming innovations is an instructional strategy that uses children's strength in decoding to help them make sense. Working together, teacher and students read a predictable story, then rewrite the story by placing different rhyming words in the structured frame.

I Was Walking down the Road, by Sarah Barchas, is an example of a book that includes many rhyming phrases that lend themselves to being rewritten. The teacher supplies the frame. For *I Was Walking down the Road*, it would look like this:

I was walking down the _____ .
I saw a little _____ .
I caught it.
I picked it up.
I put it in the cage

Prompting the students, the teacher might ask, "What are you going to pick up?" When a student suggests a cat, the teacher asks him to write the word in the second blank. The line now reads "I saw a little cat." Next, the teacher helps the children make a list of words that rhyme with "cat," such as "cat," "fat," "hat" and "rat."

Then, the teacher encourages the children to come up with a new first sentence — one that rhymes and makes sense with "I saw a little cat." The children might suggest: "I was chasing a little rat." They would write the word "rat" in the first blank and make the necessary revisions to the rest of the line. Then, they make a clean copy of the entire passage, illustrate their page and place it in a class book.

When the children generate words that rhyme, the teacher can extend their knowledge by showing how the spelling patterns can be part of longer words. For the –at sound cluster, for example, the teacher might show how words such as "cat," "fat," "chat," "rat," "bat" and "scat" are also found in longer words such as "fatter," "rattle," "battle," "scatter" and "chatting."

Activities like this enable children to use their previous knowledge of rimes to synthesize sounds that make rhymes. At the same time, however, they must also pay attention to whether the word makes sense in the context of the story.

RETELLING

When developing readers begin to read silently, they must be able to demonstrate their understanding of the story. Many struggling readers have trouble communicating this understanding without reading aloud directly from the text. They may have been so caught up in calling words that they forgot about the plot. Retelling is an instructional technique that can be used to develop an oral narration of a story.

Reminding children that stories have a beginning, middle and end, the teacher introduces a story, which the children read silently. Then the teacher encourages them to talk about the story, discussing the characters, setting, problem, main episodes and resolution. If a child has trouble doing this, the teacher can interject with prompts like, "Once there was ... who did ... in the.... This character found that....," and so on.

By retelling the story with the help of prompts or hints from the teacher, children begin to see how they can use these prompts themselves. They think about what the author told them first (setting, characters and problem), in the middle (the episodes), and at the end (resolution). This helps them develop and use their knowledge of story structure to predict what will happen next.

Like retelling, this approach begins by asking children to retell a story that has been read aloud to the whole class. It is especially useful when a story is too difficult for struggling readers to read on their own. The teacher guides the retelling by asking questions like: "Who are the characters?" "What were they doing at the beginning of the story?" "What happened next?" "How does the story end?" As the children respond, the teacher records what they are saying on chart paper. As much as possible, this summary should adhere to the natural language patterns of the students and incorporate key vocabulary and information from the original story.

When the summary is finished, the children and teacher read it together, revising anything that is unclear. The teacher then retypes it and makes a copy for each student. This becomes their reading material, which they are encouraged to read many times.

Because the summary is short and uses the children's own language, they will be able to remember the vocabulary, which will help them understand the classroom story.

STORY FRAMES

Creating story frames is another instructional technique that helps struggling readers demonstrate their understanding of stories. This particular technique, which uses a series of blanks linked by key story elements to help children focus on a particular line of thought, provides written prompts for writing a summary of narrative text.

The teacher introduces a story by inviting the children to predict what will happen. As she reads the story aloud, she stops at predetermined points to discuss the children's predictions and talk about the characters, problem and resolution. Afterwards, the teacher presents the story frame and invites the children to fill in the information. Here's an example:

56

The story took place in_____ . The main character was_____ . His problem was _____. To solve the problem, he first _____ . Next, he_____. Then, he_____ . Finally, he_____. This resolved the problem by _____ .

Using frames like this helps struggling readers define which characters and events are important to resolving the problem presented in the story. If some readers have difficulty completing part of the frame, the teacher asks them to read orally the part of the story that applies to the blank and then asks leading questions like: "If John does get the bat, what will happen? Is this a problem for John?" If this is a persistent concern, the teacher can construct a frame that emphasizes the troublesome section. The frame might be a short one like this:

In this story, the problem starts when _____ and is resolved when _____ .

This helps struggling readers focus on key aspects of story retelling. Story frames can also be used to help children generate their own stories. As students are learning how stories are formed, this technique provides them with a structure for constructing a well-formed story.

CHARACTER MAPPING

Character mapping helps struggling readers describe and remember the characters in a story by visually demonstrating their relationships and characteristics. As they read, children use the information in the text to develop their map.

The teacher introduces the main character and writes the name in the center of an overhead transparency or on the chalkboard. He then asks the children to read to find out what this character is like. They read silently to predetermined points in the story. At each predetermined stopping point, the teacher encourages to identify new character traits that have been revealed and add them to the map.

This technique helps children identify main characters and think about how their attributes influence the development of the story. When children have difficulty identifying characteristics, the teacher encourages them to read aloud sections of the story that describe the character and add this information to the map. Because a key aspect of retelling is figuring out the main characters and how they resolve conflicts, character mapping helps struggling readers with this activity. Character mapping can be extended to drawing Venn diagrams that show how characters are alike and how they're different.

REQUEST

Many struggling readers have difficulty focusing on important information, particularly when reading silently. They are often children who are great at generating questions, but don't seem concerned about the answers. In an article in *Journal of Reading*, Anthony Manzo suggests that the request technique, in which the teacher and children take turns asking and answering questions, can help improve comprehension.

The teacher introduces a story, paying particular attention to the title, then invites the children to read to a predetermined point. When this point is reached, the children play the role of teacher, asking questions about the story. As the teacher responds, he models using both information he found in the text and things he already knew to come up with his answers. After reading the next section, the teacher does the questioning by asking things like: "Who is the main character?" "What is an important event?" and "Why do you think that?" The teacher and children continue to take turns asking and answering questions until the story is finished.

Afterwards, they discuss the story as a whole, focusing on how their questions helped them sort out important information.

As children develop questions about the ideas in a story, they become more involved in thinking about meaning. Playing the role of teacher helps them construct meaning and increases their active participation in comprehending text.

GUIDED SILENT READING

Because many struggling readers don't understand the structure of the text, they may have trouble recalling a story they have read silently. The teacher can help guide their reading by providing them with opportunities to pause and discuss the story as they read.

The teacher begins by introducing the story in a way that encourages the children to focus on the key ideas. Then, as the children read, the teacher breaks the reading at appropriate points. During each pause, she may use explicit questions, a story frame, the request technique and so on. She might, for example, remind the children that the main character is important and ask them to think about what they might do in the same situation.

COMPUTER PROGRAMS

Some computer story-writing programs, such as *Storybook Weaver* (MECC) and *Kid Pix* (The Learning Company), offer prompts and pictures that help students focus on the parts of a story as they compose on the computer. This helps them understand the structure of a story.

Other programs focus on words and letters to help students ground their literacy in decoding by analogy. It is, however, very difficult to create a computer program that matches the way people think about words as they read. Still, when used in conjunction with the reading of authentic stories, these programs can help struggling readers notice letters and sounds in words. The *Academy of Reading K-3* (Autoskill) presents word-matching, sound-matching, sound-blending and sound-segmentation activities that help children understand how words work, and *Phraze Kraze* (Pettit) is a software version of *Wheel of Fortune* that helps them predict words from the letters they have identified in the words.

Spelling programs such as *Spellbound! Super Solvers* (The Learning Company) help students develop their decoding and spelling skills. Other programs, such as *Reader Rabbit II* (The Learning Company), help students figure out rhyming words using the same format as *Concentration*.

Summary

The teaching strategies suggested in this chapter illustrate activities that have been used successfully with struggling readers during the grounded phase of literacy. Most of the activities show these readers how to use textual conventions like word patterns and story structure to improve their understanding.

. . . .

EXPANDING LITERACY

During the expanding literacy phase, developing readers extend their newly acquired knowledge of word identification and word meaning to predict the meaning of words and sentences, as well as the overall meaning of a selection. By reading extensively, they encounter a variety of texts, sentence structures and word meanings. As students increase their recreational reading by reading series books and discussing them with their friends, instruction begins to focus on helping them read fluently while predicting meaning. As teachers guide reading, they encourage students to predict what will happen next.

Difficulties

Although struggling readers may display a variety of symptoms indicating that they're having trouble, the underlying problem is often a lack of fluency, both in oral reading and with developing ideas. Some struggling readers try to sound out every word individually, calling each separately and relying solely on the text to unlock meaning. The fluency of others is erratic because they don't use their knowledge of the overall story structure to check words. They, too, are caught up in the textual conventions and predict story meaning only infrequently. Still others fail entirely to use their own background knowledge to predict meaning. They decode individual words fluently but don't understand them or predict what their meaning might be in a story. As stories become more complex, these readers fail to use what they already know to predict what the text is going to say.

Instructional Strategies

For children in this phase, instructional strategies focus on encouraging them to predict sentence and story meaning. This helps them improve their reading fluency and their understanding as they read silently. To develop fluency, children read relatively familiar texts that enable them to predict sentence meaning readily.

To help developing readers learn to predict story meaning, teachers encourage them to use their understanding of the sentence structure and overall story meaning. Techniques that help children focus on developing overall story meaning are say-something sessions and literature circles. Techniques that develop fluency and encourage them to think about how sentences influence not only the meaning of a story but also the meaning of individual words are choral reading, chunking, retrospective reading, fluency development lessons, paired reading and readers' theatre. Techniques that focus on thinking only about sentences and the words in them are copy-cat stories and composing. Some computer programs also do this. At this stage, children begin to think about how sentences influence the meaning of the words and the author's intended meaning.

SAY SOMETHING

Some readers become so caught up in textual conventions that they don't think about the overall meaning of the story or use what they already know to think about what's happening in the story. Say-something sessions change the focus from reading to decode individual words to reading to say something. In their book, *Creating Classrooms for Authors*, Jerome Harste, Kathy Short and Carolyn Burke suggest that if children are invited to take turns saying something at intervals during the reading of a story, their ability to respond personally to literature will be enhanced. In addition, students will begin to read more fluently because they will be reading for their own purposes rather than the teacher's purpose.

To set the stage for "say-something" sessions, the teacher and children choose an engaging text. The teacher and one of the children — or another adult, such as a teacher's aide — demonstrate how to read with a partner and express a personal response to the text as well as how to challenge and extend the ideas of the partner.

The children then choose partners, decide whether the reading will be oral or silent, and take turns reading and saying something about what they have read. This approach focuses on reading as a social process during which understanding develops through communicating ideas to others. As they share their responses to the story, the children refine their thinking and their understanding of the story.

LITERATURE CIRCLES

Finding a purpose for reading and thinking about the ideas that might be presented in a book are difficult for struggling readers. In *Creating Classrooms for Authors*, Harste, Short and Burke suggest that literature circles help children develop their own reasons for reading by sharing their interpretations in a discussion group. As they talk about the literature, students integrate the author's ideas and concepts with their own.

For this technique to work, it is necessary to have many copies of several books on hand. The teacher holds up the books and gives a short, interesting summary of each, then invites the children to choose one to read silently. Once the reading is finished, the children who have read the same book gather in a literature circle. The teacher guides them into an open-ended discussion by issuing an invitation like: "Tell me about this book" or "Let's hear about your favorite part." At the end of the discussion, members of the group decide what they will talk about the next day. The children can also present their interpretation of the book as a "book talk."

Because this technique helps readers develop personal reasons for reading, they become more engaged. Sensitive teachers provide a range of literature so that children can select books that are familiar to them, creating a social context that encourages individual interpretations of the text. Sharing ideas in a peer group gives students an opportunity to define and elaborate on their own ideas.

Choral reading, which involves reading aloud stories or poems in unison, gives struggling readers an opportunity to follow the lead of the teacher or the group within a social context. They benefit from hearing the intonation and rhythm of a passage as more experienced readers demonstrate fluent, expressive oral reading.

The teacher and children select an engaging, but challenging, short story or poem and read it in unison. The more capable readers read ahead and slightly more loudly. All the children follow the words on the printed page. Afterwards, individual children can read the passage to the teacher who can help them with difficult words, if necessary.

This technique places reading in a social context and enables struggling readers to hear as well as read the message. It works particularly well for children who have been frustrated by their previous reading experiences. Choral reading is flexible because it can be used with any kind of text. When they experience difficulty, readers can discuss the meaning with the teacher and read the selection chorally again.

Some struggling readers don't understand that words represent thoughts. Chunking helps these children think about how words are combined to form phrases or chunks of language that mean something.

The teacher begins by explaining that reading is like thinking or talking. People talk and think in chunks of language that represent thoughts. To help readers or listeners envision a scooter, for example, we say "the red scooter" rather than "the ... red ... scooter."

Using a short story or poem, the teacher demonstrates his own phrasing while the child follows his model. Further, the teacher talks about the meaning of the phrases and how they enhance our ability to envision what's described. Then, the children are invited to read the story in chunks, imitating the teacher's model.

Chunking, then, helps children read in phrases or chunks that form thoughts. When someone has difficulty, the teacher models his own phrasing and encourages the child to imitate him immediately. If children can't hear their own non-fluent reading, the teacher can record one of their readings so they can begin to hear themselves.

RETROSPECTIVE READING

Many struggling readers are able to predict words using fairly well-developed strategies like asking themselves what would make sense in the context or taking a cue from the initial letter of a word. However, as stories become more complex, these children need to learn to check their guesses using their knowledge of word patterns and word length at the same time as they think about what makes sense in the context. Retrospective reading is a method that helps teachers talk to struggling readers about developing flexibility in the strategies they choose to predict meaning.

The child and teacher select a passage to read aloud. It should be about 100 to 200 words long and near the child's frustration reading level. The teacher listens to the first oral reading and marks miscues and evaluates fluency (1 = Slow and Word by Word; 2 = Slow and Choppy; 3 = Fluent). For a more detailed description of fluency levels, see page 102.

The miscues and fluency rating can be plotted on a graph similar to the one on the following page. The dotted line represents fluency, while the solid line represents the number of miscues.

The teacher then encourages the child to talk about the trouble-shooting strategies he could use to correct miscues. For example, the teacher might demonstrate how she would ask herself, "What would make sense in the sentence and rhymes with `man'? Oh, the word must be 'plan.'" Next, the child rereads the passage orally while the teacher marks miscues and evaluates fluency. The second oral reading is charted the same way as the first. The teacher and child then discuss the difference between the first and second readings, focusing on the strategic reading behaviors the child used the second time he read.

If the teacher considers it appropriate, she might ask the child to read the passage a third time. The results of this reading can be plotted on the graph as well.

The teacher's intervention in retrospective reading activities is critical, for she encourages children to integrate a variety of

Name _____

Fluency	Miscues	1st Reading	Intervention 2nd Reading	3rd Reading
3	1			
	2			
	3			
	4			
2	5			
	6			
	7			
	8			
	9			
1	10			

strategies by using prompts like, "What makes sense in the sentence or phrase and has the same letter pattern?" If a child is having a great deal of difficulty, the teacher may need to discuss the meaning of the selection, drawing on what the child already knows, then rephrase the prompt.

This procedure helps struggling readers focus on selecting and checking cues in order to figure out words. They learn to integrate decoding strategies by asking what would make sense in the context before checking their guess against their knowledge of words. This focus on meaning helps them develop fluency.

FLUENCY DEVELOPMENT LESSON

In an article published in the *Journal of Educational Research*, Timothy Rasinski and his colleagues developed a lesson format to help seven- to nine-year-olds in the expanding literacy phase become more fluent by reading in phrases with greater intonation and expression.

The teacher gives copies of the day's text to each student and then reads the text aloud, modeling appropriate intonation and phrasing. Next, the class discusses the content of the selection.

This important step enables children to further activate their previous knowledge of the topic, which helps them predict what the words in the passage are likely to be. Then the teacher and the children read the selection chorally several times. The children then form pairs. Each child reads the passage three times while the partner provides feedback on and positive comments about the reader's fluency. The whole class then meets again, and the teacher asks a group of two to four volunteers to read the passage aloud. Children then take the passage home and read it to family members.

PAIRED READING

Reading to a partner increases the amount of reading children do, something that is especially helpful for struggling readers. In an article in *The Reading Teacher*, Keith Topping, who has used paired reading extensively, suggests that pairing a more proficient reader with one who is less proficient helps both children improve their reading fluency and develop more positive self-concepts and attitudes toward reading. On this basis, the teacher reviews students' reading performance and assigns partners accordingly.

The partners choose a book to read aloud together and arrange a non-verbal signal, such as a nudge or squeeze, to indicate that the struggling reader is ready to proceed alone. The more proficient partner provides support by phasing in to join the reading when the struggling reader encounters difficulty. Afterwards, the two discuss what they have read. These sessions usually last 15 to 20 minutes and can easily be done at the end of the day. Reading pairs will need frequent access to the school library to select books that are familiar to both. A written handout and a demonstration of reading together makes the procedure more effective.

READERS' THEATER

Many struggling readers have difficulty because they're bound by the text and read word by word. Readers' theater, a technique that involves a dramatic reading of a play script where plot development is conveyed through the intonation, inflection and fluency of oral reading, helps them associate meaning with words.

Children begin by previewing the script and selecting roles. They then sit or stand at the front of the room and read their lines as expressively as possible. Afterwards, they discuss the content and how understanding this helped them read their part.

As the children interpret their character through oral reading, their reading becomes more fluent and they begin to read as expressively as they talk. This helps struggling readers convey meaning and overcome their tendency to read word by word. If a child has difficulty, the teacher can demonstrate how the character might say the lines. Initially, easy scripts need to be chosen so that children can read their part expressively without stumbling over words.

COPY-CAT STORIES

Some struggling readers, who are unfamiliar with the way sentence patterns influence meaning, benefit from focusing on the text in both their reading and writing. Copy-cat stories enable e students to do this by creating a new story using the words and sentence patterns of familiar predictable books. This minimizes their risk while enabling them to focus on the patterns of sentences and the way these patterns influence meaning, as well as on the way words are grouped to form meaningful ideas.

The teacher chooses a familiar book and demonstrates how to create a new story using its sentence patterns but changing either the main character or the setting. The children and teacher then create a new story together. Afterwards, each child writes her or his own version of the predictable book. The teacher encourages the students to reread their copy-cat story, which increases their fluency by helping them chunk the phrases they created in their new story.

COMPOSING

Writing stories and poems helps children focus on how words are grouped to form sentences. As a result, writing is especially important for struggling readers who may not understand how sentence patterns influence meaning. Yet these are often the very children who resist activities that involve writing. As a result, ensuring that they have an opportunity to write every day can present a challenge for teachers.

Setting aside time every day for journal or workshop writing is one way of providing this opportunity. This daily writing ensures that children will think about how language works to make meaning.

COMPUTER PROGRAMS

Many computer programs are designed specifically to help students create stories. Word processing programs such as *The Amazing Writing Machines* (Multimedia), *Magic Slate II* (Sunburst) and *Bank Street Writer III* (Scholastic) include lessons on keyboarding and enable teachers to add prompts to help students compose stories. Children who need more help may benefit from programs such as *Snoopy Writer* (American School Publishers), *Once upon a Time* (Compu-Tech)) and *Monsters and Make-Believe* (Queue), which help them form sentences, paragraphs and stories.

Another program frequently used in schools is *Accelerated Reader* (Perma-Bound), which is a management system for independent reading. Used in conjunction with regular classroom instruction, this program can increase the amount of reading children complete. It uses a point-based reward system, however, which may send the message that we read to accumulate points rather than for enjoyment.

Independent reading can be promoted without instituting a reward system. For example, inviting children who have read the same books to form discussion groups and challenging them to write questions for other students increases their motivation to read. Techniques such as these can be used alongside *Accelerated Reader*.

Summary

The teaching strategies suggested in this chapter are merely examples of some of the many effective techniques that encourage children to read fluently, predicting story meaning. Most of them show children how to use their newly acquired knowledge of textual conventions to predict word and story meaning simultaneously. By using these strategies, struggling readers expand their knowledge and use of literacy.

STRATEGIC LITERACY

During this phase, the major challenge for developing readers is to take personal control of their own reading and writing. As children begin to assume control of their own literacy development, the teacher concentrates on showing them how they constructed meaning rather than what they learned. Children are fascinated by their new knowledge and ability to control their thinking and, in fact, enjoy discussing how they arrived at answers. As they begin to assess the strategies they use to control their personal construction of meaning from text, they see all interactions from a personal point of view and experiment with their ideas about the world. Because they filter their view of the world through their own perceptions, children at this stage benefit from discussing their personal learning processes.

Difficulties

Many struggling readers continually shrug their shoulders and say "I don't know" when called on by the teacher. What they are really telling the teacher is that they don't know *how* to get an answer. As they developed as readers, they didn't spontaneously figure out the strategies involved in the reading and writing process and, as a result, they don't actively think about what they are doing. Because they are unaware of how to use strategies as they read and write, struggling readers passively read and write without constructing meaning. They become confused about the processes involved in reading and writing.

Therefore, they fall back on their strengths and rely too much either on the text or on their own previous knowledge and, subsequently, fail to monitor their own understanding. Often, they hold on to inaccurate ideas and predictions even when these are contradicted by the text because they are passively reading words hoping against hope that something will make sense. These readers need to become aware that predicting, revising their predictions and evaluating their own comprehension are strategic processes. When they are able to identify their strategies for reading and assess the strategies they use, they become more active and in control.

Instructional Strategies

Though instructional strategies may vary, at the core of each is the advancement of the reader's metacognitive attitude towards learning. Teachers can show struggling readers how to take control of their own reading by showing them what they know *before* they start reading and, *after* they have read, helping them assess what they learned.

DIRECTED READING-THINKING ACTIVITY

Because struggling readers tend to rely on the teacher to direct activities and pose questions, they are often unaware of how to make their own predictions and monitor their own understanding. Many struggling readers are reluctant to take risks because they believe that reading means getting everything right. They need to experience making predictions about a story, then confirming or rejecting these in a supportive atmosphere. This is the focus of the directed reading-thinking activity.

After choosing a book, the teacher asks the children to predict what it might be about by looking at the cover and the illustrations, and reading the title. She tries to elicit as many predictions as possible.

The teacher and children then read to predetermined points where there is just enough information to confirm or reject previous predictions. Then, the teacher uses the following questions to guide children to think about further predictions:

— What do you think is going to happen?

— How did you figure that out?
— How is your response justified?

When the end of the book is reached, teacher and children discuss the story as a whole, talking about the content as well as their predictions.

These procedures help struggling readers predict what will happen and this, in turn, encourages fluency in reading and thinking. When struggling readers have difficulty predicting, the teacher models how she figures out her own predictions and records these along with the children's so they can evaluate the process involved in constructing meaning. These strategies help struggling readers develop an active stance as they read stories.

SELF-DIRECTED QUESTIONING

Struggling readers are often confused about the process of reading. They rely too much either on the text or on their own previous knowledge to predict outcomes and, as a result, fail to monitor their own understanding. Often, they hold on to inaccurate predictions even when these are contradicted by the text. These readers need to become aware that predicting, revising their predictions and evaluating their own comprehension are active processes. Self-directed questioning is a technique that uses questions generated by the children to involve them in monitoring their own understanding.

The teacher demonstrates the active reading process by writing on the chalkboard or an overhead transparency a series of her own thoughts about a passage. These might include statements like, "I bet...," "I know that ... because the text says...," or "Oops, I knew it."

The children then read to predetermined points in a story, stopping at each point to talk about their reading. The teacher phases in to inquire about questions they asked themselves (e.g., "What can you tell yourself about your prediction?") or to model questions she asked herself as she was reading. This encourages children to use the same strategy, asking questions such as:

— What must I do? I must guess what's going to happen. I bet....

71

— What's my plan? I must use what I know. I know that....
— I wonder if it fits? I must look for hints in the text. The text says....
— Am I on the right track? I must check the text and what I know. Oops, I was wrong. That's okay, I can change my prediction. Now I bet... (or Yeah! I was right).

Afterwards, the teacher and children talk about the story and about how they constructed their responses combining what they already knew with the clues in the text. They also talk about when they changed their predictions and how often they did so. During the discussion, the teacher shares her own thought processes.

This technique helps readers not only identify how they make their predictions but also learn to assess and revise them when necessary. To do this, the teacher uses strategy-based questions like, "Does that fit your previous prediction?" "What can you tell yourself about your prediction?" "Did you use the text or your own knowledge?" and "What can you say to yourself when you change your prediction?" Because questions like these focus on monitoring comprehension rather than on coming up with right and wrong answers, they help struggling readers view reading as a process that involves actively constructing meaning. They learn that it's okay to make mistakes and revise their thinking. This is a powerful tool for passive readers who have previously regarded reading as a process that must be error-free.

EXPERIENCE-TEXT-RELATIONSHIP

Many struggling readers have difficulty making predictions using what they already know. This is especially true of children who are learning English as a second language. They may understand an experience in their own language but be unable to express this understanding in English. In an article in *The Reading Teacher*, Kathryn Au suggested using a variation of the experience-text-relationship — ETR — technique to help these readers develop active comprehension by showing them the relationships between their own experiences and what they're reading.

The teacher chooses a story and develops a plan for introducing it to the children by relating it to what they already know.

He uses broad questions to encourage them to relate their own experiences. At the end of this discussion, he guides the children to make predictions about the story using what they told him about their previous experiences.

The children then read the story, stopping at critical points to discuss how what they've read so far stacks up against their predictions and relates to their own experiences.

After the reading, the teacher guides a discussion that focuses on the children's overall understanding of the story. Then he directs the discussion to key aspects of the story that relate to the experiences the children have described, helping them express their understanding of the relationships between their own experiences and what happened in the selection.

ETR discussions proceed differently from those that often take place in typical classrooms. Initially, the teacher asks broad questions and invites all the children to talk at once to their neighbors, encouraging them to generate ideas freely in a non-judgmental atmosphere. This free-flowing generation of ideas helps the children associate their own experiences with the questions asked by the teacher. In classrooms that include students learning English as a second language, these discussions often take place in more than one language, enabling bilingual students to experiment with their own language before using English.

In this way, the technique encourages children to relate their experiences to what they read in the story and, finally, to connect these experiences with printed language. The teacher continually points out the strategic process of using what they know and their real-life experiences to figure out what the story means. In this way, he helps these students become active, strategic learners.

K-W-L TECHNIQUE

Reading informational text is often extremely difficult for struggling readers. Because they may not realize how much they already know, they often view each new reading situation as starting from scratch to learn completely unknown information. The strategic process of thinking about what they know and using this as they read informational text is foreign to many struggling readers. K-W-L, an abbreviation of What I

Know, What I *Want* to Learn, What I *Learned,* is an open-ended technique set out by Donna Ogle in an article in *The Reading Teacher.* It helps readers identify what they know and what they want to learn *before* reading a passage. *After* reading, it helps them evaluate what they actually did learn.

Beforehand, the teacher prepares worksheets containing three columns headed K — What I Know, W — What I Want to Learn and L — What I Learned. Once a topic is selected, she works with the children to brainstorm ideas about it and writes these on the chalkboard or chart paper. Then, the children write what they know under the K (What I Know) column on their own worksheet. Together, the teacher and children categorize the items in the K column and the children generate questions about the topic that they would like answered. They write these in the W (What I Want to Learn) column.

As children read the text — or various texts — silently, they add new questions to the W (What I Want to Learn) column and information to the L (What I Learned) column. After reading, they complete the L column, then work with the teacher to review the first two columns, linking what they already knew and the questions they asked with what they learned.

This technique helps children visualize concretely what they already know, the questions they have, and what they learned from text. In the process, they learn to define their own goals and assess what they're learning.

SEMANTIC MAPPING

Many struggling readers have difficulty thinking about what new words mean. They passively read these words as if this in itself will create understanding. They need to learn to use what they already know about the textual information as they read. Semantic mapping develops word meaning by visually representing the relationship between a key word and its attributes or related concepts.

The teacher begins by presenting one or two key words in the center of an overhead transparency or the chalkboard. The students brainstorm to come up with attributes of and concepts related to this word while the teacher writes what they say in a pattern resembling the spokes of a wheel. The diagram on the following page illustrates what this might look like.

74

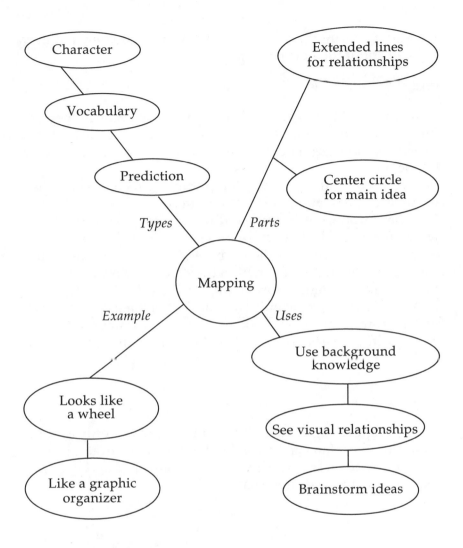

The children then read the text silently, expanding their understanding of the key words or concepts. Afterwards, they return with the teacher to the semantic map and add the newly learned information. Often, this means constructing a new map so the conceptual relationships between the key word and its attributes and related concepts are clearly delineated.

Semantic mapping helps struggling readers use what they already know as they read, then expand what they know after they read. This is important because familiarity with vocabulary is important to understanding information in content subjects. As they compare what they put on the map before and after reading, struggling readers can readily evaluate what they learned about the new concepts.

Struggling readers read and write passively because they are unaware of how to use literacy strategies. This often leads them to embrace inaccurate idea, even when these are contradicted by the text.

Several computer programs help students focus on how they formulate ideas about text. Programs like *Semantic Mapper* (Teacher Support Software) and *Inspiration* (Inspiration Software), for example, help students create written reports by reorganizing information they have gained from reading and combining this with information they already know. CD-ROMs that include content information, such as the *San Diego Zoo Presents the Animals* (Mindscape) and *Eyewitness* (DK Interactive Learning) series, are good sources of information that can be used in *Semantic Mapper*. This helps students understand how to strategically integrate information into a new whole.

Summary

The strategies suggested in this chapter represent only a few of the techniques that can be used to help develop strategic literacy. They encourage children to take control of and evaluate their own reading strategies.

. . . .

REFLECTIVE LITERACY

During this phase of literacy development, readers elaborate on their understanding of ideas from a variety of sources. They develop their understanding that some things are more important than others and select key ideas across several pieces of literature in order to summarize and remember critical information. They use these strategies to justify their own point of view and distinguish it from that of the author and other adults and students.

Reflective literacy means just what it says. Readers in this phase begin to evaluate and refine their thinking by writing about and reflecting on their ideas as they discuss and review their own thoughts and writing with the teacher and other students.

Difficulties

The students who experience difficulty during this phase of literacy are often those who try to remember everything as if it were new information. They don't use their previous knowledge of a topic to consolidate information, define its importance, and elaborate on categories of information. They also view literacy events in isolation rather than looking for patterns among ideas.

Instructional Strategies

Discussion and writing are critical to enhancing reflective thinking because these activities help students elaborate on and modify their thinking as they talk and write about their ideas. Likewise, researching and writing about ideas encourages students to expand their understanding. Strategies such as learning logs and dialogue journals help them reflect on their learning. Creating graphic organizers helps them understand relationships among concepts, while generating questions develops their ability to evaluate the importance of information.

READERS' WORKSHOP

Some struggling readers, who depend on the teacher to tell them what to look for and how to read, have trouble developing their own reasons for reading. These readers need time to read and write for their own purposes. Readers' workshop, a technique set out by Nancie Atwell in *In the Middle: Writing, Reading and Learning with Adolescents,* immerses students for several days in stories they have selected themselves. The program has several elements — mini-lessons, sustained silent reading and dialogue response journals.

For an extended period every day, students read materials they have selected themselves, keeping response journals in which they write their thoughts, feelings, questions and concerns about the book. The teacher responds in writing to the journal entries, coaching the students to think about the story and probing their thinking. For example, she might write, "I have a clear picture of the main character, but I don't understand the conflict. Can you tell me more?" In this way, she encourages the students to construct meaning.

At appropriate moments, based on her perception of the students' needs, the teacher conducts mini-lessons to demonstrate thinking processes she uses herself when reading. For example, she might talk aloud about a character's problem and how she thinks it might be solved. As she does this, she relates the character's dilemma to situations in other stories or movies. Eventually, the students begin to write entries expressing opinions based on the text and their personal knowledge.

Readers' workshops provide an excellent setting for students and teachers to reflect on how students are thinking and what sources the students are using. The dialogue journals encourage students to read for their own purposes, deciding what's important to remember and how it relates to what they already know and to other stories they have read.

OPINION-PROOF APPROACH

This approach, developed by Carol Santa, Susan Dailey and Marilyn Nelson in an article in *Journal of Reading*, engages students in reflective thinking by asking them to write opinions backed up by evidence found in a reading selection.

The teacher introduces a selection from a specific content area and invites students to think about opinions they might have about the characters or concepts presented in the passage.

After the students read the selection silently, the teacher explains the opinion-proof guide either on the chalkboard or with a handout. The guide is a sheet of paper divided into two columns. In the left column, headed Opinion, students write their opinions about characters or concepts. For example, if the passage is about amending the Constitution, the students might set out their opinion about a particular proposal. In the right column, headed Proof, students record information that justifies their opinion. While this can be drawn from their own background knowledge, it should also include information from the text. If necessary, the teacher can help them select supporting information.

After the opinion-proof guide is completed, the students use it as the basis for writing an essay that is then shared with a partner or group.

The opinion-proof approach encourages students to reflect on their ideas before a discussion takes place. Recording their thoughts helps them expand their ideas by combining information found in the text with their personal background knowledge. In this way, they learn to explain their thinking. During the follow-up discussion, they often revise their thinking, reflecting on what they wrote and how the group responded to their ideas.

LEARNING LOGS

Struggling readers sometimes become so caught up in reading and writing that they don't reflect on and evaluate their own learning. This inhibits their ability to assess their own literacy and keeps them dependent on the teacher. In *Creating Classrooms for Authors*, Jerome Harste, Kathy Short and Carolyn Burke suggest that teachers can use learning logs in a variety of content areas to help readers move towards independent, reflective thinking. Keeping logs encourages students to think and write about their learning on a daily basis. While they can write about content or processes, it is important that they review their logs as units of study wind up.

Each child needs a notebook to use as a personal learning log. As they engage in learning activities, they make entries in their logs by writing about something they're learning. These logs can be brought to discussion groups where the information they contain can be used to back up students' opinions and ideas.

Learning logs can be used in many classroom situations. For example, literature logs can be used for writing about novels or poems, while science logs can be devoted to writing about experiments or passages in textbooks. Students can keep observation logs of science activities, such as growing plants, or of social science events, such as coverage of a news item. Teachers respond to the students' log entries by encouraging them to think about how ideas relate. They might, for example, write, "I liked the observations you made, but did you ever think about how…and… are related?"

GRAPHIC ORGANIZER

Some struggling readers have difficulty organizing a mass of new information into categories and relationships; instead, they try to remember every new fact as an unrelated piece of information. As a result, they need help both to organize the new information into categories and to relate it to their background knowledge and other topics discussed in classes. Graphic organizers provide a visual representation of the main concepts in a content area. By arranging the key words in a chapter, for example, the teacher and students develop an idea framework for relating unfamiliar vocabulary and concepts.

The teacher presents the graphic organizer on the chalkboard or an overhead transparency. As he does so, he explains the relationships he is showing. Students, too, are encouraged to explain how they think the information is related. After reading a selection, students generate their own graphic organizers where they consolidate important information.

Graphic organizers are flexible and can follow a number of patterns that can depict the important relationships:

— A network tree. This places the main concepts at the top of a page, then shows subordinate information linked to the main concept in hierarchical fashion. It might be used to show, for example, the branches of government.

— Cycle frame. This shows critical events that repeat themselves in a circular chain. It might be used to show, for example, the water cycle or metamorphosis.

— Continuum. This is often used in history and mathematics to show a sequence of events or degree of measurement.

— Venn diagram. This can be used to show how concepts are interrelated as well as how they are discrete. For example, Venn diagrams that analyze main characters from different books help students see how they are alike and how they are different.

Graphic organizers help struggling readers consolidate information and organize and relate important concepts. Teachers can help students identify major headings and factual relationships by asking questions like, "Is that important information?" "Where should it go on the graphic organizer?" and "How does it relate to the other information?"

Graphic organizers also help students reflect on what they are learning and organize the information. They can lead the way to a written paragraph to further extend the student's reflective literacy. For instance, after students create a Venn diagram, the teacher might ask them to write a paragraph discussing the similarities and differences among the main characters in two books.

GENERATING QUESTIONS

Many struggling readers have difficulty identifying important information when reading textbooks or other non-fiction. Encouraging them to generate their own questions by thinking about the information that is most important in the piece helps them condense information into manageable units.

Using a short paragraph as an example, the teacher demonstrates how he makes up questions about the paragraph, stressing that the questions are about important information. Then he invites the students to read a selection silently and make up questions of their own. To follow up, the teacher and students share their questions, and the teacher provides feedback about their importance.

This strategy can also help students sort out important information in a novel. If the questions are written on cards and filed in a box, other students who read the same book can answer them in the form of a book report. Developing questions in this way helps struggling readers define important information.

COMPUTER PROGRAMS

In the reflective literacy phase, readers use many different information sources to elaborate on their understanding of ideas. CD-ROMs and the world wide web offer new ways of accessing information that can influence students' thinking. When dealing with content subjects, encyclopedias on CD-ROM, like the *World Book* and *Grolier*, offer easy ways for students to navigate through information that has been cross-referenced.

Some students find using sources such as these particularly rewarding because they perceive the volume of information on screen as more manageable, and the graphics that often accompany texts make using the information more appealing to struggling readers. As students call up links, scroll up and down, and jump from site to site at their own pace, they feel they have more control over selecting what they view as important.

Summary

The teaching strategies suggested in this chapter represent only a few of the activities that can enhance reflective thinking. They depend on students using writing as a means of reflecting on their understanding and then sharing that writing in a discussion group. This sharing encourages further reflection and rewriting.

. . . .

AN INSTRUCTIONAL

FRAMEWORK

The preceding chapters outlined an instructional framework that can be tailored to each phase of literacy development. Now it's time to incorporate these techniques into a framework for designing effective instruction that supports struggling readers as they progress through the developmental phases of literacy.

The instructional framework for a reading session is made up of four elements. The first is an easy reading activity designed to engage and warm up readers, just as stretching exercises might warm up a cross-country runner. After the warm-up comes the activity that forms the heart of the literacy event. This is a guided lesson that focuses on constructing meaning. The guided lesson is followed by strategy lessons and a writing activity. A reading session usually takes about an hour, but can be shorter or longer. Though the session might stretch over two days, it is prefereable to finish reading the story at one sitting.

If the framework is to support struggling readers, teachers must strike certain balances:

— Reading material must be both easy enough and challenging enough. Struggling readers need to read easy, familiar material that provides them with opportunities to refine and expand their repertoire of active reading strategies in situations where they can experience success. When all their reading is too easy, however, students do not develop the more sophisticated strategies required to successfully read more difficult material. When selecting reading passages, then, the teacher must strike a balance between materials that are easy and those that are challenging.

— Lessons must include both the reading of authentic literature and instruction in strategic processes. To view reading as an active process of constructing meaning, readers must read and discuss their ideas. At the same time, however, they must learn the strategies used by proficient readers. Teachers must strike a balance between using mini-lessons and demonstrations to teach strategies and ensuring that students have opportunities to focus on interpreting and understanding a story by reading authentic literature.

— Lessons must include instruction in both reading and writing. Reading and writing are mutually supportive literacy processes that bolster each other. Because struggling readers are often excused from writing activities, however, they may not benefit from the natural interaction between reading and writing. The teacher must strike a balance between these activities to ensure that children have opportunities to engage in both reading and writing.

Stage 1—Easy Reading

For four to seven minutes at the beginning of a literacy session, struggling readers read material that is easy and familiar. This enables them to relax and ease into the session. Rereading familiar selections, for example, helps children notice word and sentence patterns and discover new ways of decoding words and making meaning. Furthermore, when challenging words are encountered in a familiar context, they are easier to figure out. Beginning the literacy session with a successful reading experience also increases the children's willingness to engage in the more challenging activities that will follow.

EASY READING THROUGH THE LITERACY PHASES

During each phase of literacy development, students need time to read easy and familiar materials. Doing so helps them use what they already know to decode text and refine strategies they have developed during previous phases.

To children in the emergent literacy phase, the teacher might, for example, present three or four familiar predictable books and invite them to choose one to read aloud to an aide, a volunteer or a friend. When a child confuses or forgets words, the reading partner can simply begin reading with him until he regains the flow of the story. Reading partners can also direct children to the picture, encouraging them to use picture clues to figure out a word.

The teacher can help children in the grounded literacy phase choose an unfamiliar but easy book with readily recognizable vocabulary. When students have trouble recognizing a word in an unfamiliar book, it helps to offer support in the form of hints or prompts. Initially, the teacher might direct the child to think about the story or look at the pictures to see if this helps her figure out the unknown word. If it doesn't, the child might be asked to identify the first letter of the word. Then the teacher can ask, "What word makes sense and starts with a ...?" Providing a series of prompts helps children develop a flexible system that makes use of several different strategies to figure out a word.

Children in the expanding literacy phase can improve their fluency by reading familiar or short poems or favorite parts of chapter books. Reading with a partner is an excellent way for children to share their favorite books and encourages all students to read many easy books.

In the strategic literacy phase, the reading switches from oral to silent, which helps children refine the strategic processes they are learning. The children select the book they want to read.

In the reflective literacy phase, the teacher uses familiar quotations, newspaper articles and hot topics for the students to discuss. This emphasizes thinking fluency rather than reading fluency.

Stage 2—Guided Reading

Once the warm-up is complete, the teaching session moves on to a guided reading of new text. During this stage of the literacy event, the children read a whole story or a meaningful segment of a story. As a result, it's important to select the material carefully. Plot and character development must be readily comprehensible, and the selection should be short enough to enable the children to finish reading in one or two sessions.

The instructional sequence of a guided lesson is designed to help children construct meaning by building on what they already know and can do. As a result, before starting, teachers must ask themselves an important question: What can I do to make this story more understandable for the children? The answer helps teachers decide which key concepts to highlight *before* the children begin reading.

The teacher and students then brainstorm to develop a list of predictions related to the story theme, a technique that helps the children become actively involved in reading the story. During the reading, teacher and students pause at appropriate points to check the accuracy of the predictions. At each pause, the teacher asks open-ended questions designed to engage the students in actively reading the next segment of the selection.

Once the text has been read, the children are encouraged to respond to the story as a whole. A key element of these responses involves relating the story to their personal experiences and analyzing the effect of these experiences on their ability to comprehend the story.

GUIDED LESSONS THROUGH THE LITERACY PHASES

For children in the emergent literacy phase, predictable books make excellent reading selections and shared reading is an effective way of enjoying them. Other suggestions are found in the chapter on emergent literacy. As the children read aloud, the teacher supports them by phasing in and out of the reading as necessary. When they have trouble with words, the teacher can also prompt them to use picture clues or figure out what makes sense in the context or what fits the pattern of the words or sentences.

When the children finish reading, the teacher checks their comprehension by asking them to retell the story page by page. Not only does this reinforce textual meaning as a cue for figuring out words, but it also encourages the students to bridge the gap between meaning that is constructed within a social context and meaning that is constructed from a text.

Shared reading can also be used during the grounded literacy phase, though the material selected might switch to easy chapter or series books. These books, especially those in a series such as Frog and Toad, often incorporate the same repetitive sentence patterns as predictable books. What's more, encountering familiar characters can help struggling readers feel more comfortable about approaching unfamiliar text.

At the same time, however, chapter books provide new challenges. The sentence patterns are less rhythmic than those of predictable books and there are fewer picture clues. During this phase, teachers intensify their prompting by using a standard series of prompts that remind students to think about meaning, word patterns and letter-sound relationships. To focus on meaning, the teacher can ask whether a word makes sense or suggest that the child read the sentence again, saying a word that makes sense. To focus on word patterns, the teacher might offer clues. For example, if a child is having trouble reading the word "pan," the teacher might say, "It rhymes with 'ran.'" To focus on letter-sound knowledge, the teacher might ask, "What letter is at the beginning of that word? How do you say it?"

To help children learn these prompts on their own, reading specialists in Montana have developed the five-finger rule, which is a list of prompts that children can count off on the fingers of one hand. Holding up the first finger prompts them to think about the story, while holding up the second reminds them to check the picture for clues about what the word might be. These two prompt focus attention on meaning. Holding up the third finger reminds them to draw on their letter-sound knowledge by checking the first letter(s) of the word and pronouncing the initial letter. Holding up the fourth finger prompts them to look for chunks of letters and say a word. Holding up the thumb reminds them to ask themselves whether the word makes sense.

For children in the expanding literacy phase, the teacher uses shared reading or simply guided silent reading of chapter books. The chapter books selected can be more complex than those used during the grounded literacy phase. Books like those in the Marvin Redpost or June B. Jones series, geared to appeal to of 8- to 10-year-olds, are examples of materials that are particularly suited to children at this stage. Because the sentences in these books are longer and less predictable, they provide new challenges and help children learn to look to the sentence pattern as well as the context and letter sounds when figuring out words.

Because struggling readers are often reluctant to participate in classroom discussions, it is important for the teacher to encourage children in this phase to discuss what they are reading. As a result, the teacher's prompts should become more general than those used during earlier phases (e.g., "What is the story about?" or "What makes sense in this sentence?"). Prompts should focus on predicting meaning at the story and sentence level.

As readers' development progresses, so should the strategies used during the guided lesson. During both the strategic literacy and expanding literacy phases, it's helpful for readers to participate in literature circles where they can discuss their reading in a small group. These discussions encourage students to talk about their experiences, as well as new ideas introduced in the text, with more knowledgeable peers. As they explain their thinking, the teacher listens carefully and, when appropriate, points out the strategies they are using. Here's an example of an exchange that might take place with a child who is reading a description of Tyrannosaurus rex. The description ends with the phrase "… sharp teeth the size of bananas."

> *Child*: Whoo!!! Those are huge teeth. Huge. Imagine all those teeth. (Opens mouth wide.) I couldn't close my mouth.
> *Teacher*: You would have a mouthful. I like the way you put together what you know about bananas with the information you just read to visualize the size of the teeth.

Because it helps them integrate their thinking into a coherent whole, students in the reflective literacy stage benefit from a thematic approach to instruction. This approach enables them to draw on many different texts to develop ideas and organize and discuss their thinking. During this phase, the teacher confers with students about their progress and provides a forum in which they can share their ideas and thinking. One common forum for adolescents is a debate, which requires students to conduct research and justify their point of view on a topic of interest.

Stage 3—Strategy Lessons

During the first two stages of the reading session, teachers observe the children's strengths and weaknesses. These determine the focus of the strategy lessons, which are mini-lessons that usually last about five to seven minutes.

Because the purpose of the strategy lessons is to develop and modify the children's reading strategies, the reading material must be selected carefully. In most cases, it's a good idea to begin with easy texts. This enables the children to begin using the strategy immediately, which helps reinforce their learning. As children learn to use a strategy, more difficult material can be chosen, encouraging them to use the strategy even when the text is more challenging.

The key to designing effective strategy lessons is to ensure that the teacher has plenty of opportunity to demonstrate active reading. Rather than *telling* students how to use a strategy to figure out meaning, it's important to *show* them. This involves using I-statements to talk about the strategies as the teacher is using them. Examples of effective I-statements are included in the material that follows.

STRATEGY LESSONS THROUGH THE LITERACY PHASES

When children are in the emergent literacy phase, teachers can show them how to figure out words by looking at the pictures in the book or thinking about the entire story. If, for example, a child reading *Where the Wild Things Are* is having trouble with the word "boat," the teacher might point to the illustration and say, "In this picture, Max is traveling to where the wild things are. What is he traveling on?" When the child responds correctly, the teacher can point out: "You see? Sometimes the pictures can help you figure out the words."

In the grounded literacy phase, interactive writing can be used to write about story elements. Though the children might not know how to spell all the words, by stretching out the sounds with the teacher's help, they can write about the main character in the classroom story. The summary experience involves students in retelling a familiar story. In both cases, the teacher can demonstrate how to think about the story. If the children were summarizing the Frog and Toad story "Cookies," for example, the teacher might say something like:

"I was thinking that will power is fairly important in this story. It might be a good idea to talk about this next. Let's see, how might we say that?"

When children are in the grounded literacy phase, it is also critically important to demonstrate decoding by analogy. Word probes do this very effectively. Selecting a word from the word wall, the teacher demonstrates how to stretch out the pronunciation so that all the sounds can be heard. Then he and the students work together to create a list of rhyming words. The teacher then models how he might figure out new words by referring to the words on the list. The children follow the model and create new words that are similar to the words on the word wall.

Children in the expanding literacy phase need to understand that words can be chunked to form thought units and that the other words in a sentence can be used to decode an unknown word and predict meaning. Retrospective reading, developed from Yetta Goodman's idea of retrospective miscue analysis, is an effective technique for showing them how to do this. After students have read a selection for the first time, the teacher reviews their miscues. Before the second reading, she shows students how they can correct their mistakes by asking themselves what would make sense and looks like the word they're having trouble with. She might demonstrate her thinking by saying: "I ask myself, What would Dad use in the garden that starts with 'sh'? Maybe a shovel? When I try this word in the sentence, it reads, 'Dad shoveled the garden.' Does that make sense? Yes. I used the meaning of the sentence to fix my own mistake." The teacher would then encourage the students to continue reading, using this conversational technique when they have trouble figuring out words.

Children in the strategic literacy phase are refining their control over their own thinking and beginning to think about thinking. As a result, it is important for the teacher to show them how to analyze and assess the strategies they are using and to draw on various strategies for making sense of text.

The teacher begins by using I-statements to show students how to analyze the effectiveness of the strategies they have chosen. The purpose is to demonstrate how to move on to another strategy when one doesn't work. The students can then read with a partner, talking about the effectiveness of the strategies they are using. As the partners talk, the teacher circulates to help students name the strategies.

During the reflective literacy phase, students combine information sources to support their thinking or to refute another point of view. By demonstrating their own drafts of projects, teachers can show students how they drew on various sources to create an idea. This helps students who are using many sources of information develop their own thinking.

Stage 4—Writing Activities

Because reading and writing are based on the same system of printed words, learning to read and learning to write are processes that support each other. Both processes involve constructing meaning and checking to see whether what we are reading or writing is making sense. As we write, we must think about letters and sounds as well as meaning, just as we do when reading. Because writing helps readers focus on the printed conventions that carry meaning, it is important to include writing activities in literacy instruction. It is also important to design writing activities to support students as they move through the phases of literacy development.

WRITING ACTIVITIES THROUGH THE LITERACY PHASES

Children in the emergent literacy phase benefit from using journals to write what they know. At this stage, invented spellings are accepted — the goal is simply to encourage children to write so that they notice the letter names and sounds. Children also enjoy trading messages with a partner or writing messages to friends and family.

Framed rhyming innovations are writing activities that encourage children in the grounded literacy phase to use their knowledge of letter-sound relationships and decoding analogies. As the students create new stories using the frame of a story they have read in class, they focus on the patterns in words.

Interactive writing is another strategy that works very effectively with children in the grounded literacy phase. During an interactive writing session, the teacher has many opportunities to talk about language conventions and the letters and sounds in words.

Children in the expanding literacy phase need to develop writing fluency, which helps them develop a more integrated understanding of how sentences work and how words are put together to form chunks of language. Dialogue journals, in which students are encouraged to write about anything of interest or importance to them, are an excellent tool for promoting writing fluency. After a student's entry, the teacher comments with a brief, personal and honest reaction to what was written. For example, if a student wrote, "Today I played with my best friends and sang in the chorus concert," the teacher's response might say, "I bet you enjoyed playing with your friends. I certainly enjoy my friends." The teacher's comments can be an empathetic response, as in the previous example, or it might ask for more information (e.g., "That sounds interesting. I would like to know more about…" or "Can you explain what it felt like?"). Comments like these encourage the children to focus on recording their ideas without worrying that the mechanics of their writing are going to be evaluated.

As children move into the strategic literacy phase, they are ready to take on more sophisticated writing challenges. Writing summaries of texts they have read helps them learn to use writing to elaborate on what they are reading. At this stage of literacy development, their writing is fairly fluent and expecting them to write summaries that integrate thinking and writing is not too demanding a task. Thinking about a text and condensing the information into a short written summary requires the same kind of strategic thinking that is developing in their reading.

Readers in the reflective literacy phase are ready to reflect on their own thinking and weave ideas together into a coherent whole. Writing is an important tool for fostering the reflective thinking that occurs during this phase of their literacy development. As students read and think about a variety of texts, the teacher encourages them to make notes or brief summaries of the ideas they are encountering. These can be used later when they are combining ideas from several texts into a coherent whole.

Summary

The generic framework outlined in this chapter provides teachers a structure for planning lessons, yet enables teachers to design programs specifically for struggling readers. The framework is composed of four elements: easy reading; a guided lesson; strategy lessons; and a writing activity.

. . . .

ASSESSING LITERACY

As our view of literacy changes, so too do the techniques we use to assess this complex, dynamic process. No longer is the static measurement of skill mastery considered an adequate evaluation of literacy. When literacy is viewed as an active process of constructing meaning, in which the reader's application of skills and strategies varies with the demands of the reading situation, the assessment techniques we use must reflect this. Not only do these techniques need to be grounded in the interactive view of literacy, but they also need to focus on what readers can already do. Assessment must be continuous, using a variety of process-oriented techniques that reflect the changing nature of literacy and represent literacy development over time.

Rethinking Assessment

When selecting and creating process-oriented assessment techniques, teachers need new criteria for judging whether they are appropriate. The three questions that follow can help guide the selection process.

Is the assessment activity authentic?

Assessment tools used in classrooms must replicate real-life situations. For example, in real life, people often retell stories they have read. This means that evaluating children's retelling of stories is an authentic form of assessment. It shows children what they can already do and where they need to improve, thus

94

enhancing their ability to interact with the world at large. On the other hand, measuring children's mastery of skills that bear no resemblance to real-life situations, such as skill-and-drill exercises, is not an authentic assessment technique.

Is the assessment activity instructionally valid?

Sometimes there is a need to evaluate behaviors specific to the task of acquiring literacy. These measures provide evidence of how children are learning and thinking about a particular task or topic discussed in the classroom. This can be tricky, because the instruction must be also be valid. If the instruction focuses on a particular task that will lead to authentic literacy, then the measure is said to be instructionally valid. For instance, fluent oral reading in itself is not an authentic literacy activity because few people regularly read orally in public. However, fluent reading indicates that a child has integrated the tasks of processing both print and meaning, and this is an authentic literacy task.

Does the assessment format allow teachers to interpret children's responses consistently?

The assessment formats teachers choose help them reflect on how children are developing as literate individuals. As we observe children engaging in authentic and instructionally valid activities, we interpret the data in light of our own understanding of literacy development and the interactive view of literacy. The format we use helps us judge children's behavior in a consistent manner. For example, every time a teacher uses a checksheet to evaluate a child's retelling of a story, she must be consistent in her judgments about what counts.

Equally important is the teacher's interpretation of children's responses in light of her knowledge of literate behaviors. We must be careful not to make broad generalizations about literacy based on an assessment technique designed for a specific purpose. For example, an assessment tool that measures a child's knowledge of story structure, a single aspect of comprehension, should not be used as a basis for evaluating the child's literacy development in general.

Teachers need to select assessment tools that are authentic and instructionally valid and use them consistently. We need to remember that any assessment technique provides only a snapshot of literacy development at a particular moment. It never really captures the variety of situations that readers encounter. However, by using a variety of assessment tools in the classroom, an authentic evaluation of a student's continuing literacy development can be achieved.

This chapter suggests a variety of tools that can be used to measure literacy development during particular phases. However, their authenticity and instructional validity are not necessarily limited to a particular phase. Many can be used effectively during various stages of development. For example, because the self-assessment technique matches the developmental task of controlling learning, it appears in the section titled Strategic Literacy. However, because many children benefit from conducting self-assessments throughout their entire literacy development, its usefulness is not limited to this phase.

Emergent Literacy

During the emergent phase, readers predict the words in books based on their own knowledge and the context of the literacy event. For this reason, the tools used during this phase must be situated within an environment in which children are making sense of print. Print awareness interviews, which measure children's awareness of print, and running records, a technique that evaluates children's reading miscues, are authentic methods of assessing children's literacy and provide valuable information that can guide instruction.

PRINT AWARENESS INTERVIEW

Though various procedures have been developed for assessing young children's awareness of print, the most natural technique involves simply handing them a book — or language experience story — and asking questions. Describing their responses helps teachers evaluate how young children are developing a working knowledge of print.

— Hand a child a book or story and ask where he will begin reading. Does he know that the story begins where the print begins?
— Ask where he will go next. Does he know that the left page comes before the right? That readers move from the

top to the bottom of the page? That he should begin at the left and read along the line to the right, then return to the left margin of the next line?

— Read a line of the story and ask the child to repeat the reading. Does he know when he read too many or too few words?
— Ask him to point to a word. Does he know what a word is?
— Ask him to point to a letter and name it. Does he understand what a letter is? Can he name the letters?

RUNNING RECORDS

Teachers constantly listen to children read, deciding whether they're ready to progress to more difficult material. This simple technique was, however, obscured for a time by an overemphasis on skill development. Running records, developed by Marie Clay, are powerful tools for assessing progress and the match between reader and text.

An informal variation on Clay's system is to invite a child to read aloud a selection (about 50-100 words) and count the number of miscues. For a story to be suitable for instruction, the child should not miss more than one word in 10. If the miscue rate is higher than this, the text is too difficult and the teacher needs to find another that is less challenging.

This system also provides insights into the cueing system the child uses. Teachers can record the exact miscue and compare it to the original text, asking these questions:

— Does the word make sense?
— Does it fit grammatically in the sentence?
— Does the replacement word start with the same letter(s)?
— Does the child try to sound out the word?

As teachers listen to children read, they look for a pattern of miscues. Evaluating the cue system helps teachers match instruction to what children can already do, and analyzing the pattern of miscues provides insights into the trouble-shooting strategies children use when reading breaks down.

Grounded Literacy

Because readers use the text, both single words and story structure, to predict words and story meaning during the grounded literacy phase, assessment techniques need to reflect their growing understanding of print and story structure. Though various procedures for assessing children's knowledge of the relationship between sounds and symbols have been developed, the most natural of these involves evaluating how the child uses this system when writing. Likewise, a natural technique for evaluating comprehension is to assess the child's retelling of a story.

A spelling features assessment evaluates the child's knowledge of the relationship between sounds and symbols, while a story structure assessment evaluates comprehension. Both these tools provide valuable information about how young children cope with the conventions of print. To save time, the teacher can use the same written story summary to measure both spelling (graphophonic) awareness and story structure completeness. If these summaries are collected over the course of the school year, they can provide a concrete indication of how children's literacy development is progressing.

SPELLING FEATURES ASSESSMENT

To place the assessment of phonics knowledge in context, teachers can examine samples of children's writing, which reveals their memory for sounds in words and how these combine to form words.

The teacher selects a writing sample and scores each word according to the following scale. In each category, there is a list of the characteristics of the stage. If the student's spelling exhibits most of the characteristics, it receives the score indicated.

Pre-Sounding-Out Stage
(Score 0 for each word in this category)

— Letter forms represent a message.
— No sound-symbol relationship exhibited.
— Writes and repeats known letters fairly accurately (may have many upper-case letters).

Early Sounding-Out Stage
(Score 1 for each word in this category)

— Whole words are represented by one or more letters.
— This letter, or letters, represents some of the sounds in words, but not all.
— Letter-naming strategy is limited and random.

Sounding-Out Stage
(Score 2 for each word in this category)

— Writes a letter for more than half the sounds in the word.
— Represents sounds with a letter name (letter-naming strategy is prevalent and ordered).
— Spaces appear between most words.

Transitional Stage
(Score 3 for each word in this category)

— Letter-sound relationships based on standard spelling.
— Conventional rules are used appropriately, but not correctly (e.g., "littel" for "little").
— Reverses some letters in words.

Correct Spelling
(Score 4 for each word in this category)

— Uses conventional spelling.
— Entire word spelled correctly.

The teacher adds the scores, then finds the average by dividing the total score by the total number of words in the sample. This average helps him assess readers according to their stage of spelling (graphophonic) development. For example, if a child's average is 2.5, the teacher can indicate that she is in the sounding-out stage.

While scoring a passage using a spelling features list helps teachers analyze a child's spelling and phonics awareness, it is the evaluation process that is important rather than the score. The evaluation helps teachers identify what children can already do and monitor their developing graphophonic knowledge.

Evaluating a child's retelling of a story is a simple, authentic tool for assessing silent reading comprehension. As children retell a story orally, the teacher evaluates whether the retelling includes the setting, characters, problem, events and resolution. The same method can be used with a written summary.

The following simple format provides a quantitative score for a retelling. While it may sometimes be necessary for the teacher to provide prompts, this should be done sparingly. The idea is to evaluate each child's ability to retell the story without assistance.

Before starting, the teacher needs to analyze the story to identify the setting, problem, plot episodes and resolution. As a child retells the story, the teacher records a score for each category using the following guide.

Story Structure Assessment Rating Guide

Setting   Rating (0-4) _____

4 Includes an introduction, names of main character and other characters, description of important places and times.
3 Includes main character and some other characters, brief description of place and time.
2 Includes main character and briefly states times or place.
1 Includes only one element, such as place or names of minor characters.
0 Does not include any information related to setting.

Problem   Rating (0-4) _____

4 Includes an elaboration of the main character's primary goal or problem to be solved, including motive or theme of story. This also includes the event that sets up the problem in the story.
3 Includes primary problem main character needs to solve.
2 Includes only a sketchy idea of the problem.
1 Includes an unrelated problem.
0 Does not include problem.

Events   Rating (0-4) _____

4 Includes key events or plot episodes that lead to resolution. Most events or episodes mentioned are related to attempts

100

to solve the problem, a consequence of this action and the characters' reaction to the situation.

3 Includes some key events and some of these relate to attempts to solve the problem, a consequence of this action and the characters' reaction to the situation.

2 Includes some key events but does not elaborate on them.

1 Includes only a few unrelated events.

0 Does not include any key events.

Resolution   Rating (0-4)____

4 Ends the story so there is a sense of sequence and describes how the problem was resolved and the goal attained.

3 Ends the story so there is a sense of sequence and briefly tells how the problem was resolved.

2 Ends the story so there is a sense of sequence, but does not tell how the problem was resolved.

1 Ends the story abruptly.

0 Stops in the middle of the story.

TOTAL SCORE____

Expanding Literacy

During this phase, children read widely to develop their ability to read fluently with comprehension. Struggling readers, too, need to read widely so they can independently use the strategies learned during the first two phases of development. To help them, teachers need to match instruction to the children's strategies, evaluating their reading behavior and book selections.

FLUENCY ASSESSMENT

Equally important during this phase is the measurement of fluent oral reading. Often teachers worry unnecessarily about children's fluency during the grounded stage when, because the major task is to master the patterns of words and text, students need to read more slowly. Developing and assessing fluency becomes more important during the expanding literacy phase when assessment needs to measure whether children are spontaneously linking what words look like with what they mean in the context of the passage.

To do this, the teacher can ask children to read a paragraph aloud and rate the reading. In my own work at the reading clinic at Eastern Montana College, I found that students and teachers can successfully rate fluency using a three-point scale.

Fluency Scale

Rate 1 when reading is non-fluent, marked by word-by-word reading, numerous pauses, sound-outs and repetitions, and a lack of intonation and expression.

Rate 2 when reading is somewhat fluent with one of the following patterns:

— Slow reading in two- and three-word phrases; intonation appears choppy because of pauses to sound out or repeat words.
— Reasonable pace but improper phrasing and intonation.

Rate 3 when reading is fluent with longer phrases and good expression and intonation.

Fluent readers receive a score of three while developing readers would receive a score of two. Struggling readers who receive a score of one need more opportunities to read easy selections and hear the teacher's model.

OBSERVING BOOK SELECTIONS

One measure of children's progress towards reading fluency is the number and kinds of books they select to read independently. Teachers, parents and librarians can work together to summarize information about children's book selection habits. Some items on an observation record might include:

Book Selection Checklist

Number of books checked out ____

Number of books read ____

Rate the following on a scale of 1 to 4, with 4 meaning almost always and 1 meaning almost never.

Discussed books with friends ____

Was engaged in reading books for an extended time ____

Strategic Literacy

As children begin to control their own literacy development, teachers need to focus on *how* they construct meaning rather than on what they learn. Because an important factor in developing control is learning to evaluate oneself, children's ability to assess their own literacy development becomes critical during this phase, and it's a good idea to involve them in assessment activities.

DIRECTED READING-THINKING ACTIVITY EVALUATION

To assess a students' ability to understand stories, the teacher can evaluate their responses during a directed reading-thinking activity. The following guide can be used to create an anecdotal record of a child's responses.

DRTA Evaluation

Rate from 1 to 4:
4 indicates almost always,
1 indicates almost never.

Predictions

Makes predictions readily   ____

Uses previous experiences   ____

Uses textual information   ____

Monitoring

Checks predictions   ____

Revises predictions when necessary   ____

Justifies responses   ____

Uses previous experiences   ____

Uses text examples   ____

Rereads when necessary   ____

Extension

Can expand responses   ____

Integrates the text and previous knowledge   ____

Compares this story with others   ____

Summarizing

Important information included   ____

Critical inferences made   ____

Response well-formed   ____

QUALITATIVE ASSESSMENT OF RETELLINGS

While there is a continued emphasis on summarizing narrative and expository passages during the strategic literacy phase, evaluation focuses on the children's use of strategies to link text and background knowledge, monitor comprehension, define purposes and expand meaning.

Judy Mitchell of the University of Arizona and Pi Irwin of the Tucson Unified School District have worked extensively with the following assessment technique, which focuses on how comprehension is occurring by measuring *how* children summarized the story rather than what they said. The first four items indicate the reader's comprehension of textual information while the next four indicate metacognitive awareness, strategy use and involvement with the text. The final four items indicate facility with language and language development. These items can be rated on a scale of 1 to 4 with 4 meaning a high degree and 1 meaning none.

Process Evaluation of Retellings

The retelling:

— includes information directly stated in the text.
— includes information inferred directly or indirectly from the text.
— includes what is important to remember from the text.
— provides relevant content and concepts.
— indicates reader's attempt to connect background knowledge to text information.
— indicates reader's attempt to make summary statements or generalizations based on text that can be applied to the real world.
— indicates highly individualistic and creative impressions of or reactions to the text.

— indicates the reader's affective involvement with the text.
— demonstrates appropriate use of language (vocabulary, sentence structure, language conventions).
— indicates reader's ability to organize or compose the re-telling.
— demonstrates the reader's sense of audience or purpose.
— indicates the reader's control of the mechanics of speaking or writing.

SELF-ASSESSMENT

Because self-assessment asks children to conduct an internal dialogue about their reading strategies, this technique increases their involvement in their own learning. In a presentation to the annual convention of the International Reading Association, Susan Glazer suggested that children need a new language to talk about their own learning. This language would focus on I-statements as youngsters talk about how they are comprehending and controlling their own literacy. Teachers need to offer children consistent evaluation tools, such as checklists related to specific literacy tasks like story structure summaries, questionnaires focusing on strategies, and statements related to what they know and learned.

It's a good idea to invite children to assess themselves both before and after completing a task. For example, the K-W-L technique (where children write what they know in one column and what they learned in another) lends itself nicely to self-assessment. The teacher can draw attention to the information the student has learned through reading.

In some content-area classrooms, teachers are experimenting with open-ended questions to focus self-evaluation. They ask the children to write and respond to questions like these:

— What did I learn about sharing my ideas?
— What did I learn about putting my ideas together?
— What did I learn about the topic?

DISCUSSION GROUP ASSESSMENTS

Another way to help students reflect on their own development as readers is to invite group members to evaluate their learning as a group. This helps students look back on how they shared their knowledge and think about how their knowledge is developing. For example, individual members of a discussion group might complete the following open-ended statements:

— Something everyone in the group learned was....
— Each person learned something different. Some of the things we learned were....
— As a group, we had new questions. They were....

An activity like this helps children develop a broader perspective on their own literacy development. As they think about their own literacy and evaluate what others are learning, they refine their thinking about literacy development in general.

Reflective Literacy

During this stage, the same assessment techniques applied during other phases can be used — but in a different way. As they think about their own literacy, children, and the teacher, need to use various tools to assess their continuing development. Portfolios of children's writing about their reading are integral to assessment during this stage.

As children increasingly analyze their own development and how they synthesize and organize information, their reflective literacy is extended.

PORTFOLIO ASSESSMENT

Portfolios contain many samples of classroom work completed over an extended period. Because the work samples emerge out of classroom literacy events, they exist in context. Teaching and learning do not stop in order to assess; rather, assessment becomes integral to learning. Because it might include many drafts of a particular piece, a portfolio can demonstrate the process of learning as well as the content learned.

The reflective process involved in choosing what is included in the portfolio is the most authentic evidence of a child's learning. To each selection, children attach a paragraph explaining why it was included. As a result, when choosing what to include in their portfolios, children must reflect on their own literacy development, evaluate their learning and set new goals for themselves. In this way, portfolios are integrated into the curriculum and serve as a mirror of each child's learning.

JOURNAL ASSESSMENT

A written journal is an excellent avenue for encouraging children to reflect on how and what they are learning. Both the children and teacher can reread journal entries using a checklist to evaluate how comprehension is progressing. The following items can be rated with a Yes or No or on a graduated scale of 1 to 4.

Journal Checklist

Responses:

— are scant — single ideas and not the main one.
— become longer and more detailed over time.
— are emotional reactions.
— explain the story.
— show reasoning about the story.
— include descriptions of how comprehension is happening (e.g., describes strategies).
— show reflective development of an idea or concept.

Attitudes and Motivation

As we spend time listening to children, we get to know them in a personal way. We can deepen our knowledge of individual children's attitudes towards literacy by conducting interviews to probe this. Their responses can be very revealing.

ASSESSING ATTITUDES TOWARDS LITERACY

Questions asked during an interview might include:

— What is reading?
— What is writing?
— Who do you know who is a good reader?
— What makes him or her a good reader?
— Do you think you're a good reader? Why?
— If some friends were having trouble reading, how could you help them?

— When you're reading and come to something you don't know, what do you do?

Listening to the children helps teachers evaluate their own beliefs about literacy and the effect of these beliefs on the children's literacy development. This, in turn, helps us think about our instructional decisions and come to view these as part of the continuing assessment that happens in the classroom.

CHECKING MOTIVATION

If teachers are to develop programs that encourage children to become active readers, it's important to understand students' motivation for reading and writing. Because struggling readers tend to avoid literacy activities, their reading development does not progress at the same rate as that of their peers — often because they just don't read as much.

Questions like the following can be used to measure reading motivation in six- and seven-year-olds. The questions can be read aloud to the whole class, a small group or a single student.

— What kind of reader do your friends think you are?
— What do your best friends think about reading?
— When you are in a group talking about stories, how often do you share your ideas?
— What do you think of people who read a lot of books?
— When you come to a word you don't know, can you figure it out? How do you do that?
— When someone gives you a book for a present, how do you feel?
— When you read out loud, how do you feel?

Summary

Changes in our view of literacy have led not only to the use of assessment techniques that are authentic and instructionally valid but also to the realization that evaluation must be carried out by teachers and students, not by tests. The assessment techniques outlined in this chapter can help teachers become more reflective as we observe children learning and analyze the instructional situation. Then, we interpret the data we're collecting, giving it meaning by judging the children's behavior against our understanding of literacy development. Based on this judgment, we assess children's level of engagement in the interactive reading process and make instructional decisions.

. . . .

WORKING TOGETHER

An unfortunate by-product of our technological society has been the separation, rather than the integration, of instructional efforts. Instead of sharing expertise with one another, teachers often view themselves as marooned alone on their classroom islands. This is particularly unfortunate for struggling readers because they, above all others, could benefit from the shared expertise of the professionals within a school. Often, special programs designed for children who are experiencing reading difficulty decrease rather than increase their chances of developing literate behaviors. In addition, studies have shown that struggling readers actually receive less reading instruction than their more proficient counterparts. What's more, the quality of the instruction they do receive is often lower. It is time to devise new models that will pull together professional and community resources to provide a cohesive program for these readers.

Parents as Partners

Family experiences play an integral role in shaping children's attitudes towards literacy. In fact, most children learn to read by reading with their parents, brothers, sisters, aunts, uncles and grandparents. Although teachers can certainly provide quality literacy activities, we cannot duplicate the closeness and comfort felt by children who read and reread familiar stories with loved family members. As they read, these children also have important opportunities to discuss the stories and relate them to experiences the family has shared. When family members read together, children have a positive model that fosters their literacy development.

In homes where few family interactions center around print, however, children do not build a background of print experiences that enable them to respond naturally to classroom literacy activities. What's more, parents who have experienced stressful learning situations themselves often find it difficult to assist struggling readers. Their child's struggle brings to the surface many of the negative emotional responses and inappropriate behaviors they themselves developed in school.

There are, however, ways to work with parents to help them view literacy in a new light so that they can work successfully with their children. In England, Keith Topping and others have accomplished this by encouraging parents to sit beside their child so that they can read aloud a story together. Over time, this improves the child's reading. Others have shown parents how to use prompts that focus on meaning while reading with their children. They learn to pause, then prompt with phrases such as, "Does that make sense?" and "Read that again and see if it makes sense."

The parents were also given suggestions about when and how to provide encouragement and praise. This guidance helped them increase the amount of reading their children did each day, which improved their proficiency.

Elsewhere, parents have been invited into classrooms to share their expertise. Members of immigrant families whose children are learning English as a second language, for example, might be invited to class to share information about their language and cultural heritage. This helps their children make connections between classroom activities and family literacy and relate their home experiences more readily to things they read about at school. In addition, some schools have involved parents as tutors for struggling readers.

No matter how teachers involve parents in classroom activities, we must ensure that the activities are based on effective practices that parents can readily carry out. Furthermore, the success of programs designed to encourage parents to read with their children suggests that providing guidance in using specific techniques improves the effectiveness of these programs.

Volunteers as Reading Tutors

As education has come to be viewed as the responsibility of the entire community, schools have invited parents and community members to share in a variety of activities. Though many of these focus on fundraising, many schools have also invited volunteers to participate in tutoring programs. Every community is rich in people who can help organize and operate a volunteer tutoring program.

Often, struggling readers do not take advantage of opportunities to read in school because they lack support when difficulties arise. A volunteer tutor can fill this gap, providing the encouragement and one-to-one support needed to keep students engaged in literacy tasks and to ensure that their reading experiences are successful. The support offered may involve listening to children read familiar books or reading along with the children when the books are more challenging. This kind of support can ensure that struggling readers have the same opportunities to read as their more proficient peers.

To be an effective, however, volunteer tutors need an understanding of and training in not only specific supportive techniques but also the instructional framework that is the foundation of the classroom reading program. In addition, a supervisor knowledgeable about both reading instruction and the community may be needed. In many communities, reading specialists work closely with volunteer tutors.

Staff Review Process

Another technique for sharing expertise is the staff review process or pre-referral team. This involves a chairperson, the child's classroom teacher and a recording secretary who meet as a group to share their perspectives on a specific reader. Before the meeting, the chairperson and the classroom teacher prepare questions and collect data.

At the meeting, the classroom teacher presents the collected data, which includes information about the child's strengths, interests, behaviors, beliefs about literacy, relationships with others, and greatest needs. The group reviews the data and suggests possible strategies, building on what the child can already do. This process takes advantage of the expertise of the regular classroom teacher to solve problems in collaboration with other teachers. Decisions about children are based on data from extended observations within the context of the actual classroom.

Congruence Model

Another model that relies on the sharing of expertise is the congruence model. In their essay in *Beyond Separate Education*, Richard Allington and Anne McGill-Franzen suggest that school personnel combine their instructional practices into a unified plan for struggling readers. Like the staff review process, groups of teachers consider a child's program in a variety of instructional situations. These teachers develop a body of shared knowledge about the children, their reading instruction and the core curriculum.

Their goal is to adjust instruction so that the core curriculum in reading is accessible to all students, no matter what their reading level. Some teachers do this by inviting all students to read texts chorally. Specialists and volunteers then reread the same text with struggling readers. Other teachers create summaries of classroom stories, while still others read aloud a classroom story and encourage struggling readers to dictate their own summary of it. By repeatedly reading these summaries, the children are able to participate in class discussions and projects and eventually learn to read the class story themselves. This means that the instructional program for struggling readers is congruent with the program of instruction in the classroom.

Collaborative Education Model

Advocates of collaborative education believe that struggling readers benefit from using active reading and thinking strategies alongside their peers — and that this must occur in mainstream classrooms where these readers have appropriate role models and a chance to share their thinking. Rather than isolating struggling readers in a special classroom where a watered-down curriculum is offered, the collaborative model involves the reading specialist in supporting the efforts of struggling readers in the mainstream classroom. This means that struggling readers are constantly exposed to and challenged by the thinking of more proficient readers.

Today, the collaborative model is often adopted by entire schools. Teachers, administrators, specialists and parents share their expertise and perspectives on problems and work to reach wise solutions that everyone can view positively. Everyone involved works towards the goal of delivering high-quality instruction to all students.

In some schools, this approach has meant that teachers conduct special study classes before and after school. These classes are open to all students, not just those who are considered at risk of failing to learn. In other schools, specialists from various fields, including English as a second language and special education, team with mainstream teachers to provide support for struggling readers within the regular classroom. This may, for example, involve working with a small group of struggling readers to help them finish the assigned work at the same time as the classroom teacher is working with another group.

Summary

This chapter suggests that schools and communities share their expertise. Strategies for doing so can include welcoming parents as partners in their children's education and developing coherence among programs and collaboration among staff and community members. All the suggestions require teachers and administrators to look closely at how instruction affects struggling readers.

. . . .

A FINAL LOOK

This book has explained how reading difficulties can be attributed to a failure in the interaction between readers and their instructional environment, rather than solely to the shortcomings of a particular child. We know that many struggling readers spend less time reading and receive less reading instruction than their more proficient counterparts. The result is that they become disenchanted with school, barely scraping through. Their weak reading strategies inhibit not only their learning in school but also their ability to make a smooth transition from school to productive lives.

In this book, we've looked at how:

— the instructional program influences reading behaviors both positively and negatively at each juncture of a child's academic career. These programs need to build on the shared expertise of professionals in the school and the community.
— teachers' instructional decisions and behaviors have a powerful influence on children's learning. Instruction needs to focus on helping children construct meaning, always emphasizing making sense of stories and information.

This interactive view of literacy has tremendous implications for teachers. Some of these are summarized here.

Instructional adjustments must become the rule rather than the exception.

Many teachers find it hard to change their approach — even when it's obvious that what they're doing isn't working. What struggling readers need most is sensitive teachers who can adapt their instruction on the spot, immediately using what the children can already do to create alternative learning situations. By adjusting their instruction appropriately, teachers communicate the message that everyone is capable of learning.

Instructional decisions must be based on continuing, authentic assessment of children's progress.

As teachers become evaluators, we must continually assess how struggling readers are learning. It is necessary for us to return to the model of active literacy, evaluating how the children use many sources of information to predict meaning, check their predictions and increase their content knowledge, broaden the range of strategies they use, and expand their interpretations of the context of literacy. True and fair assessment of children's progress emerges from observations made during instruction.

Teachers must become reflective.

As we intuitively plan activities and make adjustments, we must step back from the hectic instructional day and ask ourselves, Why did I change and what did I accomplish with the change? In other words, we need to take time to make sense of our instructional decisions. As we solve these complex instructional problems, we become creators of curriculum.

We must become researchers in our own classrooms.

As we adjust our plans and assess literacy, we need to synthesize our observations about struggling readers and the instructional alternatives we create. This information becomes the research upon which to build new curriculum.

As teachers, we must ourselves become powerful models of literate behaviors.

We must read and write for our own individual purposes in the classroom. We must share our secrets about literacy and about children. As we solve complex instructional problems, we need to share our problem-solving strategies with students, parents, other teachers and administrators.

We must set sail from our classroom island to the mainland of collaborative instructional programs.

In this way, struggling readers can immerse themselves in real reading situations where they can share their interpretations with their peers.

As we work with struggling readers, we must not lose sight of the fact that, at one time, these children actively sought meaning within a literacy community. At some point in their academic careers, however, there was a mismatch between the instruction they received and their own unique strategies for constructing meaning. They experienced failure and began to struggle to make sense of what they were reading. Thereafter, these readers struggled daily to make sense, often doubting themselves and shifting blame to whomever and whatever they could in order to maintain their sense of self-worth.

We must open our minds and hearts to these children so they can feel significant in our classrooms and our lives. We must accept the legitimacy of the unique strategies they use and acknowledge that their struggle is real. But, in our compassion, we must not hook into their failure. We must create the very best instructional opportunities, giving them far more than our sympathy. We need to create instructional situations that begin with what they can already do, guiding them to expand their strategy resources. We need to listen to and support these readers as they discuss the strategies they're using and talk about how their attempts to make sense are working. We need to rejoice with them in their successes and help them celebrate their own literacy.

I hope this book helps you create instructional opportunities to transform the struggling readers in your care into readers who can again make sense of the literacy events in their lives.

. . . .

BIBLIOGRAPHY

Allington, R.L. "Oral Reading." In *Handbook of Reading Research*. P.D. Pearson, Ed. New York: Longman, 1984.

Allington, R.L. & A. McGill-Franzen. "Different Programs, Indifferent Instruction." In *Beyond Separate Education*. D. Lispsky & A. Gartner, Eds. Baltimore, Md.: Paul II. Brooks, 1989.

Almasi, J.F. "A New View of Discussion." In *Lively Discussions! Fostering Engaged Reading*. L.B. Gambrell & J.F. Almasi, Eds. Newark, Del.: International Reading Association, 1996.

Anderson, R.C., E.H. Hiebert, J.A. Scott & I.A.G. Wilkinson. *Becoming a Nation of Readers*. Washington, D.C.: National Institute of Education, 1985.

Atwell, N.M. In the Middle: *Writing, Reading and Learning with Adolescents*. Upper Montclair, N.J.: Boynton/Cook, 1987.

Au, K. "Using the Experience-Text-Relationship Method with Minority Children." In *The Reading Teacher*. Vol. 32, no. 6: 1979.

Baker, L. & A. Brown. "Metacognitive Skills and Reading." In *Handbook of Reading Research*. P.D. Pearson, Ed. New York, N.Y.: Longman, 1984.

Bristow, P.S. "Are Poor Readers Passive Readers? Some Evidence, Possible Explanations, and Potential Solutions." In *The Reading Teacher*. Vol. 39, no. 3: 1985.

Clay, M. *The Early Detection of Reading Difficulties*. Portsmouth, N.H.: Heinemann, 1985.

Dowhower, S. "Repeated Reading: Research into Practice." In *The Reading Teacher*. Vol. 42, no. 7: 1989.

Fountas, I.C. & G.S. Pinnell. *Guided Reading: Good First Teaching for All Children*. Portsmouth, N.H.: Heinemann, 1996.

Gaskins, I.W., L.C. Ehri, C. Cress, C. O'Hara & K. Donnelly. "Procedures for Word Learning: Making Discoveries about Words." In *The Reading Teacher*. Vol. 50, no. 4: 1996-1997.

Gentile, L. & M. McMillan. *Stress and Reading Difficulties*. Newark, Del.: International Reading Association, 1987.

Glazer, S.M. & L.B. Searfoss, Eds. *Reexamining Reading Diagnosis: New Trends and Procedures*. Newark, Del.: International Reading Association, 1988.

Glazer, S.M. & L.B. Searfoss. *Reading Diagnosis and Instruction: A C-A-L-M Approach*. Englewood Cliffs, N.J.: Prentice-Hall, 1988.

Goodman, Y.M. & A.M. Marek. "Retrospective Miscue Analysis." In *Retrospective Miscue Analysis: Revaluing Readers and Reading*. Y.M. Goodman & A.M. Marek, Eds. Katoneh, N.Y.: Richard C. Owen, 1996.

Harlin, R., S.E. Lipa & R. Lonberger. *The Whole Language Journey*. Scarborough, Ont.: Pippin, 1991.

Harste, J.C., K.G. Short & C. Burke. *Creating Classrooms for Authors*. Portsmouth, N.H.: Heinemann, 1988.

Johnston, P.H. & P.N. Winograd. "Passive Failure in Reading." In *Journal of Reading Behavior*. Vol. 17, no. 4: 1985.

Juel, C. "Learning to Read and Write: A Longitudinal Study of 54 Children from First through Fourth Grades." In *Journal of Educational Psychology*. Vol. 80, no. 4: 1988.

Manzo, A.V. "The Request Procedure." In *Journal of Reading*. Vol. 13, no. 2: 1969.

Mudre, L.H. & S. McCormick. "Effects of Meaning-Focused Cues on Underachieving Readers' Context Use, Self-Corrections, and Literal Comprehension." In *Reading Research Quarterly*. Vol. 24, no. 1: 1989.

Ogle, D. "K-W-L: A Teaching Model that Develops Active Reading of Expository Text." In *The Reading Teacher.* Vol. 39, no. 6: 1986.

Palinscar, A.S. & A.L. Brown. "Reciprocal Teaching of Comprehension-Fostering and Comprehension-Monitoring Activities." In *Cognition and Instruction.* Vol. 1, no. 1: 1984.

Paris, S.G. & E.R. Oka. "Strategies for Comprehending Text and Coping with Reading Difficulties." In *Learning Disability Quarterly.* Vol. 12, no. 1: 1989.

Pearson, P.D. & D.D. Johnson. *Teaching Reading Comprehension.* New York, N.Y.: Holt, Rinehart & Winston, 1978.

Raffini, J.P. *Student Apathy: The Protection of Self-Worth.* Washington, D.C.: National Education Association, 1988.

Rasinski, T., N. Padak, W. Linek & E. Sturtevant. "Effects of Fluency Development on Urban Second-Grade Readers. In *Journal of Educational Research.* Vol. 87, no. 3: 1994.

Roskos, K. & Walker, B.J. *Interactive Handbook for Reading Diagnosis.* Englewood Cliffs, N.J.: PrenticeHall/Merrill, 1994.

Santa, C.M., S.C. Dailey & M. Nelson. "Free-Response and Opinion-Proof: A Reading and Writing Strategy for Middle Grade and Secondary Teachers." In *Journal of Reading.* Vol. 28, no. 4: 1985.

Smith, F. *Joining the Literacy Club.* Portsmouth, N.H.: Heinemann, 1988.

Stanovich, K.E. "Matthew Effects in Reading: Some Consequences of Individual Differences in the Acquisition of Literacy." In *Reading Research Quarterly.* Vol. 21, no. 4: 1986.

Taylor, B.M., R.A. Short, F.J. Frye & B.A. Shearer. "Classroom Teachers Prevent Reading Failure among Low-Achieving First-Grade Students." In *The Reading Teacher.* Vol. 45, no. 8: 1992.

Topping, K. "Peer Tutoring and Paired Reading: Combining Two Powerful Techniques. In *The Reading Teacher.* Vol. 42, no. 7: 1989.

Walker, B.J. *Diagnostic Teaching of Reading: Techniques for Instruction and Assessment*. 2nd Ed. Columbus, Ohio: Merrill, 1992.

Walker, B.J. *Remedial Reading*. Washington, D.C.: National Education Association, 1990.

Will, M. *Educating Students with Learning Problems: A Shared Responsibility*. Washington, D.C.: Office of Special Education and Rehabilitative Services, U.S. Department of Education, 1986.

Wixson, K.K. & M.Y. Lipson. "Reading DisAbilities: An Interactionist Perspective." In *Contexts of School-Base Literacy*. T.E. Raphael, Ed. New York, N.Y.: Random House, 1986.

Wong, B.Y.L. "Understanding the Learning-Disabled Reader: Contribution from Cognitive Psychology." In *Topics in Learning and Learning Disabilities*. Vol. 4, no. 1: 1982.

MORE TITLES FROM THE PIPPIN TEACHER'S LIBRARY

Helping Teachers Put Theory into Practice

WRITING PORTFOLIOS
A Bridge from Teaching to Assessment

SANDRA MURPHY, MARY ANN SMITH

*How portfolios can help students become active partners
in the writing process.*

ORAL LANGUAGE FOR TODAY'S CLASSROOM

CLAIRE STAAB

*Integrating speaking and listening to help children
discover the power of language.*

THE PHONOLOGY FACTOR
Creating Balance with Beginning Readers

NADINE PEDRON/SUSAN BROWN

*How phonological awareness skills can be integrated
into literature-based, meaning-centered classrooms.*

LIFEWRITING
Learning through Personal Narrative

SYDNEY BUTLER, ROY BENTLEY

Helping students see themselves as writers.

INFOTEXT
Reading and Learning

KAREN M. FEATHERS

*Classroom-tested techniques for helping students overcome
the reading problems presented by informational texts.*

LITERACY ACTIVITIES
FOR BUILDING CLASSROOM COMMUNITIES

ARDITH DAVIS COLE

*A former "ditto queen" explains how she substituted creative
activities for boring, repetitive seatwork.*

INQUIRY IN THE CLASSROOM
Creating It, Encouraging It, Enjoying It

DAVID WRAY

How careful planning can ensure that projects become a driving force in students' learning during the early school years.

LINKING MATHEMATICS AND LANGUAGE
Practical Classroom Activities

RICHARD McCALLUM, ROBERT WHITLOW

Practical, holistic ideas for linking language — both reading and writing — and mathematics.

THE MONDAY MORNING GUIDE TO COMPREHENSION

LEE GUNDERSON

Strategies for encouraging students to interact with, rather than react to, the information they read.

AN ENGLISH TEACHER'S SURVIVAL GUIDE
Reaching and Teaching Adolescents

JUDY S. RICHARDSON

The story of an education professor who returns to a high school classroom determined to put theory into practice.

LANGUAGE, LITERACY AND CHILDREN
WITH SPECIAL NEEDS

SALLY ROGOW

How primary teachers can support children with special needs, ensuring that they are able to truly participate in mainstream classrooms.

FUSING SCIENCE WITH LITERATURE
Strategies and Lessons for Classroom Success

CARYN M. KING, PEG SUDOL

Step-by-step lesson plans for integrating literature and science with nine- to 11-year-olds.

THE FIRST STEP ON THE LONGER PATH
Becoming an ESL Teacher

MARY ASHWORTH

Practical ideas for helping children who are learning English as a second language.

For a fuller description of these and other titles, please visit Pippin's website at www.pippinpub.com

Supporting Struggling Readers

BARBARA J. WALKER

Pippin Publishing

Designed by John Zehethofer
Edited by Dyanne Rivers
Printed and bound in Canada by AGMV Marquis Imprimeur Inc.

We acknowledge the financial support of the Government of Canada
through the Book Publishing Industry Development Program for our
publishing activities.

We acknowledge the support of the Government of Ontario through the
Ontario Media Development Corporation's Ontario Book Initiative.

National Library of Canada Cataloguing in Publication

Walker, Barbara J., 1946-
    Supporting struggling readers / Barbara J. Walker; edited by Dyanne
Rivers. —2nd ed., rev. and expanded

(Pippin teacher's library ; 41)
Includes bibliographical references.
ISBN 0-88751-086-8 (pbk.)

1. Reading — Remedial teaching. I. Rivers, Dyanne. II. Title.
III. Series.

LB1050.5.W355 2003   372.43   C2003-905183-8

10 9 8 7 6 5 4 3 2

CONTENTS

. . . .

INTRODUCTION

Readers of all descriptions work to make sense of the literacy events that crowd their lives. Struggling readers, too, work to make sense of literacy events, often in situations that inhibit, rather than support, their search for meaning. Nevertheless, they *are* active learners in search of meaning who deserve support as they struggle to make sense

To help you understand and support their literacy development, this book will illustrate:

— An interactive view of the reading process.
— A developmental view of literacy.
— How inappropriate instruction can affect students' strengths and weaknesses and reinforce their reliance on ineffective learning strategies.
— Instructional methods and authentic assessment procedures that enable us to support struggling readers as they develop their literacy skills.
— An instructional framework that can be used to intervene effectively during each phase of literacy development.

In the years since this book was first published, teaching strategies and techniques have been refined and adapted to reflect new developments in the field of literacy instruction. As a result, this new, revised edition of *Supporting Struggling Readers* includes even more suggestions for helping children whose literacy development has stalled.

Furthermore, my continuing work in the field has sparked me to rework, update and shift to different chapters some of the teaching strategies included in the original edition. Though all the suggested strategies can be adapted for use at every phase of a child's literacy development, many are particularly effective when matched with specific developmental tasks. Two strategies included in the chapter dealing with strategic literacy, for example, are the directed reading-thinking activity and the experience-text relationship. They appear in this chapter because they focus on helping children integrate and elaborate on their previous knowledge as they read a text, the major developmental task of the strategic literacy phase. Both strategies can, however, also be used effectively to promote literacy development during other phases.

New teaching strategies have been added throughout the book to reflect research suggesting that word identification skills and the ability to read fluently are important elements of comprehension. We must remember, however, that children who are at risk of failing to learn to read proficiently struggle with these elements of the comprehension process. Emphasizing these strategies at the expense of strategies that encourage children to make sense when reading prevents struggling readers from demonstrating what they can do.

As you read this new edition, I hope that you will come to appreciate that struggling readers do attempt to make sense of what they read and that they do so by drawing on what they can already do. Too often, instruction focuses on what they can't do, leaving them struggling to make sense of what they're reading and writing. If teachers support the literacy development of struggling readers by joining them in focusing on what they can do, they are able to successfully construct meaning from text.